The
REVISED
Common
Lectionary

THE REVISED Common Lectionary

Consultation on Common Texts

Includes Complete List of Lections for
Years A, B, and C

Abingdon Press
Nashville

This book is printed on recycled, acid-free paper.

Library of Congress Cataloging-in-Publication Data

The Revised common lectionary 1992: the report from the Consultation
on Common Texts/Consultation on Common Texts.
    p. cm.
  Includes bibliographical references and indexes.
  ISBN 0-687-36174-5 (alk. paper)
  1. Common lectionary. 2. Lectionaries. I. Consultation on
Common Texts (Association)
BV199.L42R48 1992
264'34—dc20   92-20507
                                                       CIP

MANUFACTURED IN THE UNITED STATES OF AMERICA

CONTENTS

CONSULTATION ON COMMON TEXTS

The Consultation on Common Texts (CCT) originated in the mid-1960s as a forum for consultation on worship renewal among many Christian churches in the United States and Canada. At present, participants in the CCT include persons from the following churches or church agencies: The Anglican Church of Canada, Christian Church (Disciples of Christ), Christian Reformed Church in North America, The Episcopal Church, Evangelical Lutheran Church in America, Evangelical Lutheran Church in Canada, Free Methodist Church in Canada, International Commission on English in the Liturgy (an agency of 26 Roman Catholic national or international conferences of bishops), The Lutheran Church—Missouri Synod, Polish National Catholic Church, Presbyterian Church (U.S.A.), The Presbyterian Church in Canada, Reformed Church in America, Roman Catholic Church in the United States, Roman Catholic Church in Canada, Unitarian Universalist Christian Fellowship, The United Church of Canada, United Church of Christ, and The United Methodist Church.

The projects and publications sponsored by the Consultation include the following:

Prayers We Have in Common: This project sought to provide a contemporary ecumenical English version of prayers for the English-speaking churches around the world. Begun by the CCT, this became part of the work of the International Consultation on English Texts (ICET). These texts have now been revised by ICET's successor, the English Language Liturgical Consultation (ELLC), and published under the title *Praying Together*. The CCT continues to work with ELLC at the international level.

A Liturgical Psalter for the Christian Year, prepared and edited by Massey H. Shepherd, Jr.

Ecumenical Services of Prayer, which has been revised and will be published as *Services of Prayer*.

Common Lectionary, which has been thoroughly revised and now is reissued as the *Revised Common Lectionary*.

A Christian Celebration of Marriage: An Ecumenical Liturgy.

A Celebration of Baptism: An Ecumenical Liturgy.

Introduction

I. What Is a Lectionary?

1. A lectionary is a collection of readings or selections from the Scriptures, arranged and intended for proclamation during the worship of the People of God.

2. Lectionaries (tables of readings) were known and used in the fourth century, where major churches arranged the Scripture readings according to a schedule which follows the calendar of the church's year. Early lectionaries usually involved continuous reading, with each Sunday's texts picking up where they left off on the previous Sunday. This practice of assigning particular readings to each Sunday and festival has continued down through the history of the Christian Church. A constant pattern, however, seems to be that the later additions of special days and feasts tended to obscure the simplicity of the original Sunday texts, so that after every few centuries, the calendar needed to be simplified and pruned in order to manifest its earlier clarity.

3. Important examples of lectionaries are the Roman *Lectionary for Mass* of 1969, the *Common Lectionary* of 1983, and the *Revised Common Lectionary* of 1992. The two versions of the *Common Lectionary* are based on and derived from the Roman book.

Types of lectionaries

4. Lectionaries come in two basic forms:

a. *A simple table of readings*, which gives the liturgical day or date, and the Scripture references for the texts to be proclaimed. In this case, readings are usually proclaimed from a pulpit Bible. The *Revised Common Lectionary* is a modern example of such a table.

b. *A full-text edition*, which fleshes out the references by reprinting the specific texts from a particular translation of the Bible. Examples of this are the Roman Catholic *Lectionary for Mass*, containing the Sunday and weekday texts, and the lectionaries of the Episcopal, Lutheran, and Methodist Churches in the United States.

II. How to Use a Lectionary

5. A lectionary may be used in several ways:
a. To provide whole churches or denominations with a uniform and common pattern of biblical proclamation.

b. As a guide for clergy, preachers, church members, musicians, and Sunday school teachers, that shows them which texts are to be read on a given Sunday.

c. As a guide and resource for clergy from different local churches who wish to work and pray together as they share their resources and insights while preparing for their preaching.

d. As a resource for those who produce ecumenical preaching aids, commentaries, Sunday school curricula, and other devotional aids.

e. As a guide to individuals and groups who wish to read, study, and pray the Bible in tune with the church's prayer and preaching. Some local churches print the references to the following Sunday's readings in their bulletins and encourage people to come prepared for the next week's celebration; the psalm reference might also be included to encourage reflection on the first reading.

6. The lectionary also shows us the relationship of the readings of one Sunday with those that come before and after it. Within each of the major seasons of Lent, Easter, Advent, and Christmas-Epiphany, the flow of the season is reflected in all the Scripture texts, taken together as a set for each Sunday.

III. The Table of Readings

Finding the correct year

7. The lectionary for Sundays and major festivals is arranged in a three-year cycle. The years are known as Year A, the year of Matthew; Year B, the year of Mark; and Year C, the year of Luke.

8. The First Sunday of Advent 1992 begins a new cycle of readings: they are selected from year A, the year of Matthew, and continue until the final Sunday of the liturgical year. Then a new year begins in Advent 1993, year B, the year of Mark. Year A always begins on the First Sunday of Advent in years which can be evenly divided by three (e.g., 1992, 1995, etc.).

Year	First Sunday of Advent	Easter
A	November 29, 1992	April 11, 1993
B	November 28, 1993	April 3, 1994
C	November 27, 1994	April 16, 1995
A	December 3, 1995	April 7, 1996
B	December 1, 1996	March 30, 1997
C	November 30, 1997	April 12, 1998
A	November 29, 1998	April 4, 1999
B	November 28, 1999	April 23, 2000
C	December 3, 2000	April 15, 2001

9. At the national and international levels, individual denominations usually issue annual calendars based on the calendar of the *Common Lectionary*.

Versification

10. The numbering of verses in this table of readings follows that used in the *New Revised Standard Version* of the Bible; adaptations may be necessary if other versions of the Bible are used.

Relationship of gospel and first reading

11. From the First Sunday of Advent to Trinity Sunday of each year, the Old Testament reading is closely related to the gospel reading for the day. From the first Sunday after Trinity Sunday to Christ the King, provision has been made for two patterns of reading the Old Testament from Proper 4 [9] to Proper 29 [34].

> a. Provision of a pattern of paired readings in which the Old Testament and gospel readings are closely related. For example, in Year A, Proper 6, Exodus 19:2-8*a* and its response, Psalm 100, are used in conjunction with Romans 5:1-8 and Matthew 9:35–10:8.
>
> b. Provision of a pattern of semicontinuous Old Testament readings, such as found in Year A, Propers 7 and 8, where Genesis 21:8-21, on one Sunday, is followed by Genesis 22:1-14, the next Sunday.

For all these Sundays between Pentecost and Advent, churches and denominations may determine which of these patterns better serves their needs. Some denominations will accept one or both patterns for all their congregations; others may choose to let local liturgy planners determine which of these two patterns better serves their needs. The *Revised Common Lectionary* does not propose one set as more favored than the other, but the use of the two patterns should not be mixed.

Deuterocanonical (Apocrypha) readings

12. In all places where a reading from the deuterocanonical books (The Apocrypha) is listed, an alternate reading from the canonical Scriptures has also been provided.

Responsorial psalm

13. The psalm is a congregational response and meditation on the first reading, and is not intended as another reading. Where a choice of first readings is given, especially in the Sundays after Pentecost, the corresponding psalm or canticle should also be used.

Hallel psalms

14. Fifteen psalms (104–106, 111–113, 115–117, 135, 146–150) begin and/or end with the Hebrew "Hallelujah" ("Alleluia"; NRSV translation, "Praise the Lord"). These Hallel psalms play a particular role in Jewish liturgy, especially in the feast of

the Passover. Whenever a portion of a Hallel psalm is appointed by the *Revised Common Lectionary,* the versification indicates that it is desirable to include the "Hallelujah" ("Alleluia") or "Praise the Lord" which begins and/or ends the psalm. It may also be used as a refrain after each verse or set of verses.

Introducing readings

15. In the opening verses of readings, when a pulpit Bible is used, the reader should omit initial conjunctions which refer only to what has preceded, and substitute nouns for pronouns when the person referred to is not otherwise clear. The reader may also preface the reading with an introduction, such as "N. said (to N.)."

Length

16. When appropriate, readings may be shortened or lengthened, with discretion. Suggested longer readings are indicated by the verses in parentheses.

Two numbering systems

17. Users should follow one of the two numbering systems provided for the Propers. The Arabic numbers without brackets begin on the Sixth Sunday after the Epiphany. This method gives fixed monthly dates (with a six-day cycle) for each set of readings. The bracketed numbers [-] refer to the systems used by the Roman Catholic Church and The Anglican Church of Canada, based on the Roman lectionary. The differing numbers do not indicate differing readings.

18. To assist all denominations, the dates between which the readings may occur (on the Sundays after Pentecost) are also provided.

IV. Using the Revised Common Lectionary

19. The *Revised Common Lectionary* and its earlier edition of 1983 continue the pattern of the Roman *Lectionary for Mass* of 1969. The 1992 revision follows the basic calendar of the Western church, provides for a three-year cycle of three readings, and allows the sequence of gospel readings each year to lead God's people to a deeper knowledge of Christ and faith in him. It is the paschal mystery of the saving death and resurrection of the Lord Jesus that is proclaimed through the lectionary readings and the preaching of the Church.

20. Except for occasional changes, the *Revised Common Lectionary* accepts the *cornerstone* of the Roman lectionary: the semicontinuous reading of the three synoptic gospels over a three-year period. This pattern connects the first reading with the gospel for the Sundays after Epiphany and Pentecost. The Old Testament passage is perceived as a parallel, a contrast, or as a type leading to its fulfillment in the gospel. The *Revised Common Lectionary* provides two approaches to the first reading for the Sundays after Pentecost: one set of Old Testament readings continues the Roman

lectionary pattern, while the other offers a series of semicontinuous passages, allowing a larger variety of particular Old Testament themes to be presented.

Calendar

21. Lectionary tables and calendars are always interconnected. At the heart of the particular way each calendar sets out its selected readings is a very basic view about our faith and our Christian way of life. The *Revised Common Lectionary* has taken the present Western calendar for Sundays, has simplified it to a certain extent by moving away from some recurring annual festivals with their distinctive themes, and has returned to a pattern of continuous or semicontinuous reading in one system for successive Lord's Days after Pentecost.

22. The *Revised Common Lectionary* calendar contains both festival Sundays around the celebrations of Easter and Christmas, and the ordinary Sundays following the feasts of Epiphany and Pentecost. These are described in the following notes.

A three-year cycle of Sunday readings

23. The lectionary provides a three-year plan or pattern for the Sunday readings. Each year is centered on one of the synoptic gospels. Year A is the year of Matthew, Year B is the year of Mark, and Year C is the year of Luke. John is read each year, especially in the times around Christmas, Lent, and Easter, and also in the year of Mark, whose gospel is shorter than the others. The three synoptic evangelists have particular insights into Christ. Each year, we allow one of these gospels to lead us to Christ by a semicontinuous reading during the Sundays in Ordinary Time. Passages and parables that are unique to one evangelist are normally included as part of the Sunday readings.

Easter cycle

24. The *Revised Common Lectionary*, along with its Roman parent, emphatically relates the gospels for the Sundays of Lent with the Easter proclamation. This is particularly true in year A, where the baptismal emphasis is strong. These Sundays relate closely to the primary Lenten theme, preparation for the joy of Easter, rather than to a penitential note. On the Sunday before Easter, known as Palm or Passion Sunday, it is recommended that both the story of the palm procession and the passion narrative be used. For some Christians, this marks a significant reform of liturgical praxis in providing a balanced experience and understanding of the whole event of Jesus' suffering, death, and resurrection.

25. A final concern in relation to the Easter cycle has to do with the disuse of the Hebrew Scriptures during the season of Easter in the Roman lectionary (a practice mentioned by Augustine in the fifth century). Following the liturgical tradition of the Ambrosian and Hispanic rites in the West and also that of the majority of the Churches in the East, the Roman lectionary of 1969 does not use the Old Testament

during the Great Fifty Days from Easter to Pentecost. Nevertheless, the Roman rite has included extensive Old Testament readings in the vigils for Easter and Pentecost. The *Revised Common Lectionary* has, however, provided alternate Old Testament readings for those feasts and rubrics which provide for the unvarying use on those festivals of crucial readings from the Acts of the Apostles as the second reading.

26. As Acts becomes the first reading on these great Sundays, the apostolic reading (epistle) is taken from 1 Peter, the letters of John, and the book of Revelation. The purpose of this selection is to complement the Acts narrative of the formation and growth of the resurrection community with a theological commentary on the character of its inner life, namely, its mutual love, and its life of praise in anticipation of the fulfillment of the kingdom.

Christmas cycle

27. The structure of the Christmas cycle presumes an Advent which is basically eschatological (looking forward to the return or second coming of the Lord Jesus and the realization of the reign of God) more than a season of preparation for Christmas (which recalls his first coming among us). In the readings, Isaiah is prominent, along with Jeremiah, Malachi, Zephaniah, Micah, and 2 Samuel. The gospels of the first Sunday in each year are all apocalyptic; those of the second and third Sundays refer to the preaching and ministry of John the Baptist. On the Fourth Sunday of Advent the annunciation of the birth of Christ is proclaimed.

28. On the Epiphany, the gospel of the sages from the East is read. The Sunday after the Epiphany has the Baptism of the Lord as its theme. The rubrics of the *Revised Common Lectionary* make provision to ensure the celebration of the Lord's baptism when the Epiphany is celebrated on the Sunday after January 6. The *Revised Common Lectionary* leaves the last Sunday after Epiphany, the Sunday before Lent begins, open to two different centuries-old traditions: provision has been made for reading the Transfiguration gospel either on the last Sunday after Epiphany or on the Second Sunday of Lent. The underlying issue here is whether or not the Sundays after Epiphany are regarded as a season with an Epiphany theme (the manifestation or revelation of God), or simply, as in the Roman calendar, the beginning of the Sundays in Ordinary Time, which will resume their sequence after Pentecost.

Sundays during the year

29. The *Revised Common Lectionary* adopts the plan used in the Roman calendar, whereby "Ordinary Time" is the period outside the seasons of Lent and Easter, Advent and Christmas. The 33 or 34 Sundays which fall in the periods after the Baptism of the Lord and after Pentecost form a distinct sequence, and are guided by the gospel of the year.

30. In the Roman lectionary, the readings for the Sundays in Ordinary Time do not form a complete set, as they do during the Easter and Christmas cycles. The operative principle of selection is a semicontinuous pattern of readings from the

synoptic gospels week by week; the more ancient lectionaries also tended to use continuous or semicontinuous readings. Although the Roman lectionary works this way with the New Testament and gospel readings, it chooses the Old Testament passage for its close relationship with the gospel of the day (see Luke 24:26-27, 44-47; John 5:39; Acts 28:23). During the Sundays after the Epiphany, the *Revised Common Lectionary* continues this pattern.

31. It is at this point that the *Revised Common Lectionary* begins to vary from the Roman pattern: two distinct systems are offered for the Sundays after Pentecost (Propers 4-29). While system 2 continues the Roman pattern, system 1 applies the semicontinuous method to the first reading as well (in a sense, carrying out the logic of the Roman model more consistently than it has done itself).

32. The principle of the continuous reading of biblical books functions in other ways as well. Just as the ordinary Sundays are the occasion for reading the synoptic gospels over three successive years, so also are these same gospels used largely for the festival Sundays and seasons, although there the fourth gospel will also be found. Similarly, over the three-year cycle of the lectionary, those same Sundays will provide worshippers with most of the important texts of the Pauline corpus. In some seasons, certain books are read intensively, such as Isaiah in Advent and the letters of John and Peter, Revelation, and Acts in the season of Easter. The significance of this principle is that the biblical books are read in such a way as to permit them to contextualize themselves. Surely this is a matter of some importance, especially in terms of homiletical assumptions.

Using the lectionary in worship

33. The Roman lectionary is, as its official title indicates, a "Lectionary for Mass." Both the gospel-oriented character of the Roman lectionary and the comparative brevity of its readings show that it is intended for use in a liturgy of the word within the celebration of the eucharist.

34. The *Revised Common Lectionary* is intended for a wider ecumenical audience and will be used in many churches whose worship on the Lord's Day is at times celebrated as a complete liturgy of the word without a eucharist. In such cases the use of the lectionary will be more directly homiletical but this is not inconsistent with its purpose.

35. In preparing this revision of the *Common Lectionary*, the task force was conscious of this agenda for preaching, and of the need for the three readings and the psalm to carry the weight of an entire service of the word, as distinguished from a celebration of "word and sacrament." Accordingly, many readings for the Sundays after Pentecost have been lengthened. And of course, this was at least a part of the decision to replace the Old Testament readings of the Roman lectionary in Ordinary Time with a further semicontinuous track in each of the three years. This reflects a long-standing and greatly loved tradition in Protestant churches of preaching which focuses entirely on the Old Testament or the epistle, the same being true in the Anglican tradition of Morning Prayer with a sermon.

36. The weekly use of an appointed psalm is helpful. Sometimes the psalm has been regarded simply as another Old Testament reading (often said responsively). The *Common Lectionary* has enabled churches to recover the practice of sung psalmody on a weekly basis, as an inspection of the Presbyterian and United Methodist hymnals in the United States will show.

37. Another benefit of the arrangement of the three readings, especially in Ordinary Time, is to provide those who must plan ahead for worship—preachers, musicians, and graphic artists—with a rich prospectus well in advance so that those biblical motifs can find their way into hymns, anthems, banners, vestments, and paraments, as well as sermons. Such a use may seem to promote thematic celebrations, but that is already true by intent even of the Roman system during the major seasons of the year. In the *Revised Common Lectionary* on the Sundays after Pentecost, the sequence of three separate "tracks" of semicontinuous readings acts as a certain restraint on such a tendency.

38. The sequence of readings for Ordinary Time, however, especially in the *Common Lectionary*, provides perhaps the most important emphasis on Christian worship: the primacy of the Lord's Day. As the ancient cornerstone of the Christian calendar, it stands forth particularly in the way in which the Lord's word is proclaimed Sunday by Sunday. The *Common Lectionary* and its revision have strengthened this important recovery of the way in which the community of Christ thinks of itself "in time" and also in anticipation of the fulfillment of time at the end of its sequence of Lord's Days, namely, the *Day of the Lord!*

Fourth gospel

39. Although it is not given a year of its own, the gospel of John is used during the major seasons, the so-called "festal" days of the year. Some see the inner outline of this gospel as an attempt to provide a Christian understanding of the great festivals of the Jewish calendar; it is certainly not a sequential, chronological narration as much as it is a liturgical, theological exposition of the paschal mystery. Others would understand the gospel of John as being catechetical or mystogogical, since it examines what it means to be the community of Jesus Christ; in this interpretation, the symbolism of the Jewish feasts is seen as illustrative. The *Revised Common Lectionary* seeks to read the four gospels during the liturgy in a manner which respects their own varied literary structures.

Use of the Old Testament

40. The *Revised Common Lectionary* diverges considerably from the assumptions regarding the use of the Old Testament contained in its denominational predecessors. The 1978 Washington consultation that began the process that resulted in *Common Lectionary* (1983) raised serious questions about the Roman lectionary's "typological" use of the books of the Hebrew Scriptures. This raises what is, in a way, the enduring theological issue with which Paul struggled throughout his ministry and

epistles, that of the relationship of the Christian community to its Jewish parentage. Related questions have to do with Jesus as Messiah, the Church as the New Israel, and the authority of the Old Testament in the Christian Church today.

41. In the second century, Marcion questioned the place of the Old Testament in the Christian Church. From time to time throughout Christian history, there have been people who have echoed this position. Today's Christian Church fully accepts the Jewish Scriptures—our Old Testament—as the word of God, recognized by Jesus and the apostles and the early Christians. We have to admit, however, that throughout the centuries, many Western eucharistic lectionaries have not included Old Testament readings for Sunday eucharist. A much better balance is being achieved in today's lectionaries.

42. The Consultation on Common Texts undertook to address this biblical-liturgical problem. The dimensions of the task may be described in terms of a number of options which should probably be avoided. One extreme would be, as in the past practice of the West, to ignore the Old Testament on Sunday by leaving it only to the daily office. Another error, in the estimation of many, would be to read it only as a kind of completed or fulfilled prophecy which has been "superseded" by the New Testament Church and its writings, rather than reading and exegeting it as Scripture in its own right, rite, and historical context. However, it is surely not theologically permissible to read the Old Testament at eucharistic worship, or Christian worship in general, as though there were no linkage with Christian belief and prayer. If so, then how should that linkage be symbolized and expressed?

43. The Consultation on Common Texts in 1983 revised the Roman lectionary's handling of the Sundays after Pentecost (in Ordinary Time) in order to provide an alternative to the week-by-week correlation of gospel reading and Old Testament passage. It did this by way of a broader concept of correlation having to do with the Old Testament concerns of the three synoptic gospels. It was decided to play out the logic of semicontinuous reading in terms of the Old Testament lessons as well as the second readings taken from the New Testament.

44. When the Consultation on Common Texts turned to an extensive evaluation of its 1983 edition in preparation for a revised edition, it was this aspect of its work which created the greatest interest and drew the most careful correspondence. Some critics wondered about the desirability of long narrative passages, which seemed to them to be pushing the liturgy of the word in the direction of didacticism and Bible study. On the other hand, those who had long used the Old Testament narratives and the prophetic voices as basic to their social stance found *Common Lectionary* a great improvement and encouragement.

Alternative series of first readings

45. Several of the member Churches of CCT, notably the Roman Catholic, Lutheran, and Episcopal Churches, have followed the tradition of relating the first lesson closely to the gospel reading for the day. The *Common Lectionary* (1983) had

largely departed from this practice, as already noted, in the Sundays after Pentecost. The *Revised Common Lectionary* has provided an alternate set of first readings for the Sundays after Pentecost, to meet the desire of these traditions that the eucharistic liturgy and its readings be unified around the paschal mystery as it is proclaimed in the gospel reading. In almost every case, these readings have been selected from the options presently available in the Roman Catholic, Episcopal, and Lutheran lectionaries. This series of thematic readings shares equal status with the broader thematic semicontinuous series of readings.

46. As the decline of biblical literacy proceeds apace, among adults as well as young Christians, the return to a greater selection of readings from the Bible may be the most important gift of these Roman and Common systems for the public proclamation of the word of God. At last we have recovered a liturgical way to lead the faithful followers of Christ through his birth, baptism, ministry, death, and resurrection, which is precisely what the sacraments have also sought to do. The paschal mystery begins, in its earthly way, at Bethlehem, and traces its ways through the events of God's acts of salvation in Jesus Christ. This is the story the synoptic gospels tell.

V. Introducing the Three Years

Year A

47. Year A focuses on the gospel of Matthew. The gospel readings from the season of Advent through the Sundays after the Epiphany tell of the coming of Christ and his manifestation especially through his preaching. Most of the first readings, chosen to illuminate the gospel passage, are from the prophet Isaiah. The second readings include selections mainly from Romans and 1 Corinthians. The season also features some traditional propers, such as John 1 on Christmas Day. Churches may conclude the period after Epiphany with a reading on the Transfiguration, unless this gospel text is to be proclaimed on the Second Sunday in Lent.

48. From Ash Wednesday through Pentecost of year A, we continue to focus on Matthew. Many of the gospel readings, however, are traditional selections from the gospel of John, including the three great initiatory texts of John 4, 9, and 11 on Lent 3, 4, and 5, and the discourses of John during the season of Easter. During the season of Lent, the first readings are chosen to illuminate the gospel, and include important narratives of faith. During the season of Easter, the first readings are from Acts. The second readings highlight Romans and the initiatory exhortations in 1 Peter.

49. During the Sundays after Pentecost, the gospel readings move forward through the gospel of Matthew. One set of Old Testament lessons is a semicontinuous series of readings that focus on the major Genesis narratives, the covenant with Moses, and the establishment of Israel in the promised land. The other set of readings is selected from throughout the Hebrew Scriptures for their relationship with the

gospel of the day. The second readings are taken from Romans, Philippians, and 1 Thessalonians. The final Sundays after Pentecost focus on eschatological themes and the reign of Christ.

Year B

50. Year B focuses on the gospel of Mark. The gospel readings from the season of Advent through the Sundays after Epiphany tell of the coming of Christ and his ministry. The first readings, chosen to illuminate the gospel, are selected from throughout the Old Testament. The second readings include selections mainly drawn from the two letters to the Corinthians.

51. From Ash Wednesday through Pentecost of year B, we add readings from John and Luke to the readings from Mark. During the season of Lent, the first readings, chosen to illuminate the gospel, include important narratives of faith. During the season of Easter the first readings are from Acts. The second readings during this season are a semicontinuous selection from 1 John.

52. During the Sundays after Pentecost, the gospel readings move forward through the gospel of Mark, with five Sundays from John 6 to supplement the list. One set of Old Testament lessons is a series of semicontinuous readings that focus on the Davidic covenant and Wisdom literature, while the other set is selected from throughout the Hebrew Scriptures because of their close relationship with the gospel of the day. The second readings are semicontinuous selections from 2 Corinthians, Ephesians, James, and Hebrews. The final Sundays after Pentecost focus on eschatological themes and the reign of Christ.

Year C

53. Year C focuses on the gospel of Luke. The gospel readings from the season of Advent through the Sundays after Epiphany tell of the coming of Christ and the beginning of Jesus' ministry. The first readings, chosen to illuminate the gospels, are selected from throughout the Hebrew Scriptures. The second readings include semicontinuous readings from 1 Corinthians.

54. From Ash Wednesday through Pentecost of year C, we add several readings from John to those of Luke. During the season of Lent, the first readings, chosen to illuminate the gospel, include both narrative and prophetic passages. During the season of Easter, semicontinuous selections are read from the book of Revelation.

55. During the Sundays after Pentecost, the gospel readings move forward through the gospel of Luke. One set of Old Testament texts is a series of semicontinuous readings of the prophetic proclamation, chosen in chronological order and highlighting Jeremiah. The other set of readings is selected from throughout the Jewish Scriptures for their close relationship with the gospel of the day. The second readings are semicontinuous selections, chosen mainly from Galatians, Colossians, 1 and 2 Timothy, and 2 Thessalonians. The final Sundays after Pentecost focus on eschatological themes and the reign of Christ.

Holy Week

56. For all three years, the readings appointed for Holy Week focus on the last days of Jesus' life in the flesh (see Hebrews 5:7). The readings appointed for the Easter Vigil, following ancient tradition, include narratives and poems from the Old Testament which describe the history of salvation and the Christian passage from death to life in baptism.

TITLES OF SUNDAYS AND SPECIAL DAYS

The following is a list of the Sundays and Special Days included in the *Revised Common Lectionary*. Each Church may then choose how to name each set of Sundays and Special Days, and whether or not to include all of these days in its own lectionary.

SEASON OF ADVENT

First Sunday of Advent	Sunday between November 27 and December 3
Second Sunday of Advent	Sunday between December 4 and December 10
Third Sunday of Advent	Sunday between December 11 and December 17
Fourth Sunday of Advent	Sunday between December 18 and December 24

SEASON OF CHRISTMAS

Nativity of the Lord (Christmas Day)	December 25
First Sunday after Christmas	Sunday between December 26 and January 1
New Year's Day	January 1
Second Sunday after Christmas	Sunday between January 2 and January 5

SEASON OF EPIPHANY (ORDINARY TIME)*

Epiphany of the Lord	January 6 or First Sunday in January
First Sunday after the Epiphany [1] (Baptism of the Lord)	Sunday between January 7 and January 13

Second Sunday after the Epiphany [2]	Sunday between January 14 and January 20
Third Sunday after the Epiphany [3]	Sunday between January 21 and January 27
Fourth Sunday after the Epiphany [4]	Sunday between January 28 and February 3
Fifth Sunday after the Epiphany [5]	Sunday between February 4 and February 10
Sixth Sunday after the Epiphany [6] (Proper 1, except when this Sunday is the Last Sunday after the Epiphany)	Sunday between February 11 and February 17
Seventh Sunday after the Epiphany [7] (Proper 2, except when this Sunday is the Last Sunday after the Epiphany)	Sunday between February 18 and February 24
Eighth Sunday after the Epiphany [8] (Proper 3, except when this Sunday is the Last Sunday after the Epiphany)	Sunday between February 25 and February 29
Ninth Sunday after the Epiphany [9] (Proper 4, for Churches that do not observe the Last Sunday after the Epiphany with Transfiguration readings)	Sunday between March 1 and March 7
Last Sunday after the Epiphany (Transfiguration Sunday)	

Season of Lent

Ash Wednesday

First Sunday in Lent

Second Sunday in Lent

Third Sunday in Lent

Fourth Sunday in Lent

Fifth Sunday in Lent

Sixth Sunday in Lent (Passion Sunday or Palm Sunday)

Holy Week
　　Monday of Holy Week
　　Tuesday of Holy Week
　　Wednesday of Holy Week

Holy Thursday
Good Friday
Holy Saturday

SEASON OF EASTER

Resurrection of the Lord
  Easter Vigil
  Easter Day

Second Sunday of Easter

Third Sunday of Easter

Fourth Sunday of Easter

Fifth Sunday of Easter

Sixth Sunday of Easter

Ascension of the Lord
  (Fortieth day, Sixth Thursday of Easter)

Seventh Sunday of Easter

Day of Pentecost

SEASON AFTER PENTECOST (ORDINARY TIME)*

Trinity Sunday
(First Sunday after Pentecost)

Second through Twenty-Sixth Sunday after Pentecost
  (Propers 4-28 [9-33])

Reign of Christ or Christ the King   Sunday between November 20 and
  Last Sunday after Pentecost   November 26
  (Proper 29 [34])

SPECIAL DAYS

February 2—Presentation of the Lord

March 25—Annunciation of the Lord

May 31—Visitation of Mary to Elizabeth

September 14—Holy Cross

November 1—All Saints

Fourth Thursday of November (U.S.), Second Monday of October (Can.)
  —Thanksgiving Day

*Note: Since Easter is a moveable feast, it can occur as early as March 22 and as late as
April 25. When Easter is early, it encroaches on the Sundays after the Epiphany,

reducing their number, as necessary, from as many as nine to as few as four. In similar fashion, the date of Easter determines the number of Sunday Propers after Pentecost. When Easter is as early as March 22, the numbered Proper for the Sunday following Trinity Sunday is Proper 3.

The Propers in [brackets] indicate the Proper numbering system of the Roman Catholic Church and The Anglican Church of Canada.

Year A

Begins on the First Sunday of Advent in 1992, 1995, 1998, 2001, 2004.

SEASON OF ADVENT

First Sunday of Advent

Isaiah 2:1-5
Psalm 122
Romans 13:11-14
Matthew 24:36-44

Second Sunday of Advent

Isaiah 11:1-10
Psalm 72:1-7, 18-19
Romans 15:4-13
Matthew 3:1-12

Third Sunday of Advent

Isaiah 35:1-10
Psalm 146:5-10
  or Luke 1:47-55
James 5:7-10
Matthew 11:2-11

Fourth Sunday of Advent

Isaiah 7:10-16
Psalm 80:1-7, 17-19
Romans 1:1-7
Matthew 1:18-25

SEASON OF CHRISTMAS

Nativity of the Lord
  (Christmas Day)

> Any of the following three Propers may be used on Christmas Eve/Day.

The readings from Propers II and III for Christmas may be used as alternatives for Christmas Day. If Proper III is not used on Christmas Day, it should be used at some service during the Christmas cycle because of the significance of John's prologue.

Christmas, Proper I (A, B, C)	Isaiah 9:2-7
	Psalm 96
	Titus 2:11-14
	Luke 2:1-14 (15-20)
Christmas, Proper II (A, B, C)	Isaiah 62:6-12
	Psalm 97
	Titus 3:4-7
	Luke 2:(1-7) 8-20
Christmas, Proper III (A, B, C)	Isaiah 52:7-10
	Psalm 98
	Hebrews 1:1-4, (5-12)
	John 1:1-14

First Sunday after Christmas Day

The following readings are used on the First Sunday after Christmas unless the readings for the Epiphany of the Lord are preferred.

	Isaiah 63:7-9
	Psalm 148
	Hebrews 2:10-18
	Matthew 2:13-23
January 1—Holy Name of Jesus (Mary, Mother of God) (A, B, C)	Numbers 6:22-27
	Psalm 8
	Galatians 4:4-7 or Philippians 2:5-11
	Luke 2:15-21
January 1—When observed as New Year's Day (A, B, C)	Ecclesiastes 3:1-13
	Psalm 8
	Revelation 21:1-6a
	Matthew 25:31-46

Second Sunday after Christmas Day (A, B, C)

The following readings are provided for use when Epiphany (January 6) is celebrated on a weekday following the Second Sunday after Christmas Day.

> Jeremiah 31:7-14
>   or Sirach 24:1-12
> Psalm 147:12-20
>   or Wisdom of Solomon 10:15-21
> Ephesians 1:3-14
> John 1:(1-9), 10-18

SEASON OF EPIPHANY (ORDINARY TIME)

Epiphany of the Lord (A, B, C)	Isaiah 60:1-6 Psalm 72:1-7, 10-14 Ephesians 3:1-12 Matthew 2:1-12
Baptism of the Lord [1] (First Sunday after the Epiphany)	Isaiah 42:1-9 Psalm 29 Acts 10:34-43 Matthew 3:13-17
Second Sunday after the Epiphany [2]	Isaiah 49:1-7 Psalm 40:1-11 1 Corinthians 1:1-9 John 1:29-42
Third Sunday after the Epiphany [3]	Isaiah 9:1-4 Psalm 27:1, 4-9 1 Corinthians 1:10-18 Matthew 4:12-23
Fourth Sunday after the Epiphany [4]	Micah 6:1-8 Psalm 15 1 Corinthians 1:18-31 Matthew 5:1-12
Fifth Sunday after the Epiphany [5]	Isaiah 58:1-9*a*, (9*b*-12) Psalm 112:1-9 (10) 1 Corinthians 2:1-12, (13-16) Matthew 5:13-20

Sixth Sunday after the Epiphany [6]

> *Proper 1.* If this is the Sunday before Ash Wednesday, this Proper may be replaced, in those Churches using Transfiguration readings on this day, by the readings for the Last Sunday after the Epiphany.

> Deuteronomy 30:15-20
> or Sirach 15:15-20
> Psalm 119:1-8
> 1 Corinthians 3:1-9
> Matthew 5:21-37

Seventh Sunday after the Epiphany [7]

Proper 2. If this is the Sunday before Ash Wednesday, this Proper may be replaced, in those Churches using Transfiguration readings on this day, by the readings for the Last Sunday after the Epiphany.

> Leviticus 19:1-2, 9-18
> Psalm 119:33-40
> 1 Corinthians 3:10-11, 16-23
> Matthew 5:38-48

Eighth Sunday after the Epiphany [8]

Proper 3. If this is the Sunday before Ash Wednesday, this Proper may be replaced, in those Churches using Transfiguration readings on this day, by the readings for the Last Sunday after the Epiphany.

> Isaiah 49:8-16*a*
> Psalm 131
> 1 Corinthians 4:1-5
> Matthew 6:24-34

Ninth Sunday after the Epiphany [9]

Proper 4. The following readings are for Churches whose calendar requires this Sunday, and do not observe the Last Sunday after the Epiphany as Transfiguration.

> Deuteronomy 11:18-21, 26-28
> Psalm 31:1-5, 19-24
> Romans 1:16-17; 3:22*b*-28, (29-31)
> Matthew 7:21-29

Last Sunday after the Epiphany
(Transfiguration Sunday)

The following readings are used in Churches where the Last Sunday after the Epiphany is observed as Transfiguration Sunday.

> Exodus 24:12-18
> Psalm 2
> or Psalm 99
> 2 Peter 1:16-21
> Matthew 17:1-9

SEASON OF LENT

Ash Wednesday (A, B, C)	Joel 2:1-2, 12-17
	or Isaiah 58:1-12
	Psalm 51:1-17
	2 Corinthians 5:20*b*–6:10
	Matthew 6:1-6, 16-21
First Sunday in Lent	Genesis 2:15-17; 3:1-7
	Psalm 32
	Romans 5:12-19
	Matthew 4:1-11
Second Sunday in Lent	Genesis 12:1-4*a*
	Psalm 121
	Romans 4:1-5, 13-17
	John 3:1-17
	or Matthew 17:1-9
Third Sunday in Lent	Exodus 17:1-7
	Psalm 95
	Romans 5:1-11
	John 4:5-42
Fourth Sunday in Lent	1 Samuel 16:1-13
	Psalm 23
	Ephesians 5:8-14
	John 9:1-41
Fifth Sunday in Lent	Ezekiel 37:1-14
	Psalm 130
	Romans 8:6-11
	John 11:1-45

Sixth Sunday in Lent
(Passion Sunday or Palm Sunday)

> Those who do not observe the procession with palms and do not wish to use the passion gospel may substitute the gospel and psalm given for the Liturgy of the Passion with the gospel and psalm indicated for the Liturgy of the Palms. Whenever possible, the whole passion narrative should be read.

Liturgy of the Palms   Matthew 21:1-11
                                        Psalm 118:1-2, 19-29

Liturgy of the Passion   Isaiah 50:4-9*a*
                                        Psalm 31:9-16
                                        Philippians 2:5-11
                                        Matthew 26:14–27:66
                                          or Matthew 27:11-54

HOLY WEEK

Monday of Holy Week (A, B, C)   Isaiah 42:1-9
                                        Psalm 36:5-11
                                        Hebrews 9:11-15
                                        John 12:1-11

Tuesday of Holy Week (A, B, C)   Isaiah 49:1-7
                                        Psalm 71:1-14
                                        1 Corinthians 1:18-31
                                        John 12:20-36

Wednesday of Holy Week (A, B, C)   Isaiah 50:4-9*a*
                                        Psalm 70
                                        Hebrews 12:1-3
                                        John 13:21-32

Holy Thursday (A, B, C)   Exodus 12:1-4, (5-10), 11-14
                                        Psalm 116:1-2, 12-19
                                        1 Corinthians 11:23-26
                                        John 13:1-17, 31*b*-35

Good Friday (A, B, C)   Isaiah 52:13–53:12
                                        Psalm 22
                                        Hebrews 10:16-25
                                          or Hebrews 4:14-16; 5:7-9
                                        John 18:1–19:42

Holy Saturday (A, B, C)

The following readings are for use at services other than the Easter Vigil.

                                        Job 14:1-14
                                          or Lamentations 3:1-9, 19-24
                                        Psalm 31:1-4, 15-16
                                        1 Peter 4:1-8
                                        Matthew 27:57-66
                                          or John 19:38-42

SEASON OF EASTER

Resurrection of the Lord
Easter Vigil (A, B, C)

> The following readings and psalms are provided for use at the Easter Vigil. A minimum of three Old Testament readings should be chosen. The reading from Exodus 14 should always be used.

Old Testament Readings
and Psalms (A, B, C):

Genesis 1:1–2:4a
  Psalm 136:1-9, 23-26
Genesis 7:1-5, 11-18; 8:6-18; 9:8-13
  Psalm 46
Genesis 22:1-18
  Psalm 16
Exodus 14:10-31; 15:20-21
  Exodus 15:1b-13, 17-18
Isaiah 55:1-11
  Isaiah 12:2-6
Baruch 3:9-15, 32–4:4
  or Proverbs 8:1-8, 19-21; 9:4b-6
  Psalm 19
Ezekiel 36:24-28
  Psalm 42 and 43
Ezekiel 37:1-14
  Psalm 143
Zephaniah 3:14-20
  Psalm 98

New Testament Reading
(A, B, C):

Romans 6:3-11
  Psalm 114

Gospel:

Matthew 28:1-10

Resurrection of the Lord
Easter Day

First Reading:

Acts 10:34-43
  or Jeremiah 31:1-6
Psalm 118:1-2, 14-24

Second Reading:

Colossians 3:1-4
  or Acts 10:34-43

Gospel:

John 20:1-18
  or Matthew 28:1-10

Easter Evening (A, B, C)

The following readings are for occasions when the main (eucharistic) Easter service must be late in the day. They are not intended for Vespers (Evening Prayer) on Easter Evening.

Isaiah 25:6-9
Psalm 114
1 Corinthians 5:6b-8
Luke 24:13-49

Second Sunday of Easter

Acts 2:14a, 22-32
Psalm 16
1 Peter 1:3-9
John 20:19-31

Third Sunday of Easter

Acts 2:14a, 36-41
Psalm 116:1-4, 12-19
1 Peter 1:17-23
Luke 24:13-35

Fourth Sunday of Easter

Acts 2:42-47
Psalm 23
1 Peter 2:19-25
John 10:1-10

Fifth Sunday of Easter

Acts 7:55-60
Psalm 31:1-5, 15-16
1 Peter 2:2-10
John 14:1-14

Sixth Sunday of Easter

Acts 17:22-31
Psalm 66:8-20
1 Peter 3:13-22
John 14:15-21

Ascension of the Lord (A, B, C)

These readings may also be used on the Seventh Sunday of Easter.

Acts 1:1-11
Psalm 47
  or Psalm 93
Ephesians 1:15-23
Luke 24:44-53

Seventh Sunday of Easter

Acts 1:6-14
Psalm 68:1-10, 32-35
1 Peter 4:12-14; 5:6-11
John 17:1-11

Day of Pentecost

If the passage from Numbers is chosen for the First Reading, the passage from Acts is used as the Second Reading.

First Reading:

Acts 2:1-21
or Numbers 11:24-30
Psalm 104:24-34, 35b

Second Reading:

1 Corinthians 12:3b-13
or Acts 2:1-21

Gospel:

John 20:19-23
or John 7:37-39

SEASON AFTER PENTECOST (ORDINARY TIME)

Trinity Sunday
(First Sunday after Pentecost)

Genesis 1:1–2:4a
Psalm 8
2 Corinthians 13:11-13
Matthew 28:16-20

If the Sunday between May 24 and 28 inclusive follows Trinity Sunday, the Proper for the Eighth Sunday after the Epiphany [8] is used.

Proper 4 [9]
Sunday between
May 29 and June 4 inclusive
(if after Trinity Sunday)

| Genesis 6:9-22; 7:24; 8:14-19 | or | Deuteronomy 11:18-21, 26-28 |
| Psalm 46 | | Psalm 31:1-5, 19-24 |

Romans 1:16-17; 3:22b-28, (29-31)
Matthew 7:21-29

Proper 5 [10]
Sunday between
June 5 and June 11 inclusive
  (if after Trinity Sunday)

Genesis 12:1-9	or Hosea 5:15–6:6
Psalm 33:1-12	Psalm 50:7-15

Romans 4:13-25
Matthew 9:9-13, 18-26

Proper 6 [11]
Sunday between
June 12 and June 18 inclusive
  (if after Trinity Sunday)

Genesis 18:1-15, (21:1-7)	or Exodus 19:2-8*a*
Psalm 116:1-2, 12-19	Psalm 100

Romans 5:1-8
Matthew 9:35–10:8, (9-23)

Proper 7 [12]
Sunday between
June 19 and June 25 inclusive
  (if after Trinity Sunday)

Genesis 21:8-21	or Jeremiah 20:7-13
Psalm 86:1-10, 16-17	Psalm 69:7-10, (11-15), 16-18

Romans 6:1*b*-11
Matthew 10:24-39

Proper 8 [13]
Sunday between
June 26 and July 2 inclusive

Genesis 22:1-14	or Jeremiah 28:5-9
Psalm 13	Psalm 89:1-4, 15-18

Romans 6:12-23
Matthew 10:40-42

Proper 9 [14]
Sunday between
July 3 and July 9 inclusive

    Genesis 24:34-38, 42-49, 58-67   or   Zechariah 9:9-12
    Psalm 45:10-17   Psalm 145:8-14
      or Song of Solomon 2:8-13

            Romans 7:15-25*a*
            Matthew 11:16-19, 25-30

Proper 10 [15]
Sunday between
July 10 and July 16 inclusive

    Genesis 25:19-34   or   Isaiah 55:10-13
    Psalm 119:105-112   Psalm 65:(1-8), 9-13

            Romans 8:1-11
            Matthew 13:1-9, 18-23

Proper 11 [16]
Sunday between
July 17 and July 23 inclusive

    Genesis 28:10-19*a*   or   Wisdom of Solomon 12:13, 16-19
    Psalm 139:1-12, 23-24   or Isaiah 44:6-8
            Psalm 86:11-17

            Romans 8:12-25
            Matthew 13:24-30, 36-43

Proper 12 [17]
Sunday between
July 24 and July 30 inclusive

    Genesis 29:15-28   or   1 Kings 3:5-12
    Psalm 105:1-11, 45*b*   Psalm 119:129-136
      or Psalm 128

            Romans 8:26-39
            Matthew 13:31-33, 44-52

Proper 13 [18]
Sunday between
July 31 and August 6 inclusive

    Genesis 32:22-31   or   Isaiah 55:1-5
    Psalm 17:1-7, 15   Psalm 145:8-9, 14-21

            Romans 9:1-5
            Matthew 14:13-21

Proper 14 [19]
Sunday between
August 7 and August 13 inclusive

       Genesis 37:1-4, 12-28   or   1 Kings 19:9-18
       Psalm 105:1-6, 16-22, 45*b*   Psalm 85:8-13

               Romans 10:5-15
               Matthew 14:22-33

Proper 15 [20]
Sunday between
August 14 and August 20 inclusive

       Genesis 45:1-15   or   Isaiah 56:1, 6-8
       Psalm 133   Psalm 67

               Romans 11:1-2*a*, 29-32
               Matthew 15:(10-20), 21-28

Proper 16 [21]
Sunday between
August 21 and August 27 inclusive

       Exodus 1:8–2:10   or   Isaiah 51:1-6
       Psalm 124   Psalm 138

               Romans 12:1-8
               Matthew 16:13-20

Proper 17 [22]
Sunday between
August 28 and September 3 inclusive

       Exodus 3:1-15   or   Jeremiah 15:15-21
       Psalm 105:1-6, 23-26, 45*c*   Psalm 26:1-8

               Romans 12:9-21
               Matthew 16:21-28

Proper 18 [23]
Sunday between
September 4 and September 10 inclusive

       Exodus 12:1-14   or   Ezekiel 33:7-11
       Psalm 149   Psalm 119:33-40

               Romans 13:8-14
               Matthew 18:15-20

Year A

Proper 19 [24]
Sunday between
September 11 and September 17 inclusive

    Exodus 14:19-31   or   Genesis 50:15-21
    Psalm 114   Psalm 103:(1-7), 8-13
     or Exodus 15:1b-11, 20-21

        Romans 14:1-12
        Matthew 18:21-35

Proper 20 [25]
Sunday between
September 18 and September 24 inclusive

    Exodus 16:2-15   or   Jonah 3:10–4:11
    Psalm 105:1-6, 37-45   Psalm 145:1-8

        Philippians 1:21-30
        Matthew 20:1-16

Proper 21 [26]
Sunday between
September 25 and October 1 inclusive

    Exodus 17:1-7   or   Ezekiel 18:1-4, 25-32
    Psalm 78:1-4, 12-16   Psalm 25:1-9

        Philippians 2:1-13
        Matthew 21:23-32

Proper 22 [27]
Sunday between
October 2 and October 8 inclusive

    Exodus 20:1-4, 7-9, 12-20   or   Isaiah 5:1-7
    Psalm 19   Psalm 80:7-15

        Philippians 3:4b-14
        Matthew 21:33-46

Proper 23 [28]
Sunday between
October 9 and October 15 inclusive

    Exodus 32:1-14   or   Isaiah 25:1-9
    Psalm 106:1-6, 19-23   Psalm 23

        Philippians 4:1-9
        Matthew 22:1-14

Proper 24 [29]
Sunday between
October 16 and October 22 inclusive

Exodus 33:12-23   or   Isaiah 45:1-7
Psalm 99   Psalm 96:1-9, (10-13)

1 Thessalonians 1:1-10
Matthew 22:15-22

Proper 25 [30]
Sunday between
October 23 and October 29 inclusive

Deuteronomy 34:1-12   or   Leviticus 19:1-2, 15-18
Psalm 90:1-6, 13-17   Psalm 1

1 Thessalonians 2:1-8
Matthew 22:34-46

Proper 26 [31]
Sunday between
October 30 and November 5 inclusive

Joshua 3:7-17   or   Micah 3:5-12
Psalm 107:1-7, 33-37   Psalm 43

1 Thessalonians 2:9-13
Matthew 23:1-12

Proper 27 [32]
Sunday between
November 6 and November 12 inclusive

Joshua 24:1-3*a*, 14-25   or   Wisdom of Solomon 6:12-16
Psalm 78:1-7   or Amos 5:18-24
                                        Wisdom of Solomon 6:17-20
                                         or Psalm 70

1 Thessalonians 4:13-18
Matthew 25:1-13

Proper 28 [33]
Sunday between
November 13 and November 19 inclusive

Judges 4:1-7   or   Zephaniah 1:7, 12-18
Psalm 123   Psalm 90:1-8, (9-11), 12

1 Thessalonians 5:1-11
Matthew 25:14-30

Proper 29 [34]
(Reign of Christ or Christ the King)
Sunday between
November 20 and November 26 inclusive

Ezekiel 34:11-16, 20-24	or	Ezekiel 34:11-16, 20-24
Psalm 100		Psalm 95:1-7a

Ephesians 1:15-23
Matthew 25:31-46

All Saints	Revelation 7:9-17
November 1 or the	Psalm 34:1-10, 22
First Sunday in November	1 John 3:1-3
	Matthew 5:1-12

Thanksgiving Day	Deuteronomy 8:7-18
Fourth Thursday in November	Psalm 65
(U.S.)	2 Corinthians 9:6-15
Second Monday in October (Can.)	Luke 17:11-19

YEAR B

Begins on the First Sunday of Advent in 1993, 1996, 1999, 2002, 2005.

SEASON OF ADVENT

First Sunday of Advent

Isaiah 64:1-9
Psalm 80:1-7, 17-19
1 Corinthians 1:3-9
Mark 13:24-37

Second Sunday of Advent

Isaiah 40:1-11
Psalm 85:1-2, 8-13
2 Peter 3:8-15*a*
Mark 1:1-8

Third Sunday of Advent

Isaiah 61:1-4, 8-11
Psalm 126
    or Luke 1:47-55
1 Thessalonians 5:16-24
John 1:6-8, 19-28

Fourth Sunday of Advent

2 Samuel 7:1-11, 16
Luke 1:47-55
    or Psalm 89:1-4, 19-26
Romans 16:25-27
Luke 1:26-38

SEASON OF CHRISTMAS

Nativity of the Lord
  (Christmas Day)

Any of the following three Propers may be used on Christmas Eve/Day.

The readings from Propers II and III for Christmas may be used as alternatives for Christmas Day. If Proper III is not used on Christmas Day, it should be used at some service during the Christmas cycle because of the significance of John's prologue.

Christmas, Proper I (A, B, C)	Isaiah 9:2-7 Psalm 96 Titus 2:11-14 Luke 2:1-14, (15-20)
Christmas, Proper II (A, B, C)	Isaiah 62:6-12 Psalm 97 Titus 3:4-7 Luke 2:(1-7), 8-20
Christmas, Proper III (A, B, C)	Isaiah 52:7-10 Psalm 98 Hebrews 1:1-4, (5-12) John 1:1-14

First Sunday after Christmas Day

The following readings are used on the First Sunday after Christmas unless the readings for the Epiphany of the Lord are preferred.

	Isaiah 61:10–62:3 Psalm 148 Galatians 4:4-7 Luke 2:22-40
January 1—Holy Name of Jesus (Mary, Mother of God) (A, B, C)	Numbers 6:22-27 Psalm 8 Galatians 4:4-7 or Philippians 2:5-13 Luke 2:15-21
January 1—When observed as New Year's Day (A, B, C)	Ecclesiastes 3:1-13 Psalm 8 Revelation 21:1-6a Matthew 25:31-46

Second Sunday after Christmas Day (A, B, C)

The following readings are provided for use when Epiphany (January 6) is celebrated on a weekday following the Second Sunday after Christmas Day.

Jeremiah 31:7-14
or Sirach 24:1-12
Psalm 147:12-20
or Wisdom of Solomon 10:15-21
Ephesians 1:3-14
John 1:(1-9), 10-18

Season of Epiphany (Ordinary Time)

Epiphany of the Lord (A, B, C)

Isaiah 60:1-6
Psalm 72:1-7, 10-14
Ephesians 3:1-12
Matthew 2:1-12

Baptism of the Lord [1]
(First Sunday after the Epiphany)

Genesis 1:1-5
Psalm 29
Acts 19:1-7
Mark 1:4-11

Second Sunday after the Epiphany [2]

1 Samuel 3:1-10, (11-20)
Psalm 139:1-6, 13-18
1 Corinthians 6:12-20
John 1:43-51

Third Sunday after the Epiphany [3]

Jonah 3:1-5, 10
Psalm 62:5-12
1 Corinthians 7:29-31
Mark 1:14-20

Fourth Sunday after the Epiphany [4]

Deuteronomy 18:15-20
Psalm 111
1 Corinthians 8:1-13
Mark 1:21-28

Fifth Sunday after the Epiphany [5]

Isaiah 40:21-31
Psalm 147:1-11, 20c
1 Corinthians 9:16-23
Mark 1:29-39

Sixth Sunday after the Epiphany [6]

> *Proper 1.* If this is the Sunday before Ash Wednesday, this Proper
> may be replaced, in Churches using Transfiguration readings on this
> day, by the readings for the Last Sunday after the Epiphany.

2 Kings 5:1-14
Psalm 30
1 Corinthians 9:24-27
Mark 1:40-45

Seventh Sunday after the Epiphany [7]

Proper 2. If this is the Sunday before Ash Wednesday, this Proper may be replaced, in those Churches using Transfiguration readings on this day, by the readings for the Last Sunday after the Epiphany.

Isaiah 43:18-25
Psalm 41
2 Corinthians 1:18-22
Mark 2:1-12

Eighth Sunday after the Epiphany [8]

Proper 3. If this is the Sunday before Ash Wednesday, this Proper may be replaced, in those Churches using Transfiguration readings on this day, by the readings for the Last Sunday after the Epiphany.

Hosea 2:14-20
Psalm 103:1-13, 22
2 Corinthians 3:1-6
Mark 2:13-22

Ninth Sunday after the Epiphany [9]

Proper 4. The following readings are for Churches whose calendar requires this Sunday, and do not observe the Last Sunday after the Epiphany as Transfiguration.

Deuteronomy 5:12-15
Psalm 81:1-10
2 Corinthians 4:5-12
Mark 2:23–3:6

Last Sunday after the Epiphany
(Transfiguration Sunday)

The following readings are used in Churches where the Last Sunday after the Epiphany is observed as Transfiguration Sunday.

2 Kings 2:1-12
2 Corinthians 4:3-6
Psalm 50:1-6
Mark 9:2-9

SEASON OF LENT

Ash Wednesday (A, B, C)	Joel 2:1-2, 12-17 or Isaiah 58:1-12 Psalm 51:1-17 2 Corinthians 5:20*b*–6:10 Matthew 6:1-6, 16-21
First Sunday in Lent	Genesis 9:8-17 Psalm 25:1-10 1 Peter 3:18-22 Mark 1:9-15
Second Sunday in Lent	Genesis 17:1-7, 15-16 Psalm 22:23-31 Romans 4:13-25 Mark 8:31-38 or Mark 9:2-9
Third Sunday in Lent	Exodus 20:1-17 Psalm 19 1 Corinthians 1:18-25 John 2:13-22
Fourth Sunday in Lent	Numbers 21:4-9 Psalm 107:1-3, 17-22 Ephesians 2:1-10 John 3:14-21
Fifth Sunday in Lent	Jeremiah 31:31-34 Psalm 51:1-12 or Psalm 119:9-16 Hebrews 5:5-10 John 12:20-33

Sixth Sunday in Lent
(Passion Sunday or Palm Sunday)

> Those who do not observe the procession with palms and do not wish to use the passion gospel may substitute the gospel and psalm given for the Liturgy of the Passion with the gospel and psalm indicated for the Liturgy of the Palms. Whenever possible, the whole passion narrative should be read.

Liturgy of the Palms

Mark 11:1-11
or John 12:12-16
Psalm 118:1-2, 19-29

Liturgy of the Passion

Isaiah 50:4-9*a*
Psalm 31:9-16
Philippians 2:5-11
Mark 14:1–15:47
or Mark 15:1-39, (40-47)

HOLY WEEK

Monday of Holy Week (A, B, C)

Isaiah 42:1-9
Psalm 36:5-11
Hebrews 9:11-15
John 12:1-11

Tuesday of Holy Week (A, B, C)

Isaiah 49:1-7
Psalm 71:1-14
1 Corinthians 1:18-31
John 12:20-36

Wednesday of Holy Week (A, B, C)

Isaiah 50:4-9*a*
Psalm 70
Hebrews 12:1-3
John 13:21-32

Holy Thursday (A, B, C)

Exodus 12:1-4, (5-10), 11-14
Psalm 116:1-2, 12-19
1 Corinthians 11:23-26
John 13:1-17, 31*b*-35

Good Friday (A, B, C)

Isaiah 52:13–53:12
Psalm 22
Hebrews 10:16-25
or Hebrews 4:14-16; 5:7-9
John 18:1–19:42

Holy Saturday (A, B, C)

The following readings are for use at services other than the Easter Vigil.

Job 14:1-14
or Lamentations 3:1-9, 19-24
Psalm 31:1-4, 15-16

1 Peter 4:1-8
Matthew 27:57-66
or John 19:38-42

SEASON OF EASTER

Resurrection of the Lord
Easter Vigil (A, B, C)

The following readings and psalms are provided for use at the Easter
Vigil. A minimum of three Old Testament readings should be chosen.
The reading from Exodus 14 should always be used.

Old Testament Readings
and Psalms (A, B, C):

Genesis 1:1–2:4a
Psalm 136:1-9, 23-26
Genesis 7:1-5, 11-18; 8:6-18; 9:8-13
Psalm 46
Genesis 22:1-18
Psalm 16
Exodus 14:10-31; 15:20-21
Exodus 15:1b-13, 17-18
Isaiah 55:1-11
Isaiah 12:2-6
Baruch 3:9-15, 32–4:4
or Proverbs 8:1-8, 19-21; 9:4b-6
Psalm 19
Ezekiel 36:24-28
Psalm 42 and 43
Ezekiel 37:1-14
Psalm 143
Zephaniah 3:14-20
Psalm 98

New Testament Reading
(A, B, C):

Romans 6:3-11
Psalm 114

Gospel:

Mark 16:1-8

Resurrection of the Lord
Easter Day

First Reading:

Acts 10:34-43
or Isaiah 25:6-9
Psalm 118:1-2, 14-24

Second Reading: 1 Corinthians 15:1-11
                                   or Acts 10:34-43

Gospel: John 20:1-18
                                   or Mark 16:1-8

Easter Evening (A, B, C)

   The following readings are for occasions when the main (eucharistic)
   Easter service must be late in the day. They are not intended for
   Vespers (Evening Prayer) on Easter Evening.

                                   Isaiah 25:6-9
                                   Psalm 114
                                   1 Corinthians 5:6*b*-8
                                   Luke 24:13-49

Second Sunday of Easter   Acts 4:32-35
                                   Psalm 133
                                   1 John 1:1–2:2
                                   John 20:19-31

Third Sunday of Easter   Acts 3:12-19
                                   Psalm 4
                                   1 John 3:1-7
                                   Luke 24:36*b*-48

Fourth Sunday of Easter   Acts 4:5-12
                                   Psalm 23
                                   1 John 3:16-24
                                   John 10:11-18

Fifth Sunday of Easter   Acts 8:26-40
                                   Psalm 22:25-31
                                   1 John 4:7-21
                                   John 15:1-8

Sixth Sunday of Easter   Acts 10:44-48
                                   Psalm 98
                                   1 John 5:1-6
                                   John 15:9-17

Ascension of the Lord (A, B, C)

   These readings may also be used on the Seventh Sunday of Easter.

Year B

>Acts 1:1-11
>Psalm 47
> or Psalm 93
>Ephesians 1:15-23
>Luke 24:44-53

Seventh Sunday of Easter

>Acts 1:15-17, 21-26
>Psalm 1
>1 John 5:9-13
>John 17:6-19

Day of Pentecost

If the passage from Ezekiel is chosen for the First Reading, the passage from Acts is used as the Second Reading.

First Reading:

>Acts 2:1-21
> or Ezekiel 37:1-14
>Psalms 104:24-34, 35b

Second Reading:

>Romans 8:22-27
> or Acts 2:1-21

Gospel:

>John 15:26-27; 16:4b-15

SEASON AFTER PENTECOST (ORDINARY TIME)

Trinity Sunday
  (First Sunday after Pentecost)

>Isaiah 6:1-8
>Psalm 29
>Romans 8:12-17
>John 3:1-17

If the Sunday between May 24 and 28 inclusive follows Trinity Sunday, the Proper for the Eighth Sunday after the Epiphany [8] is used.

Proper 4 [9]
Sunday between
May 29 and June 4 inclusive
  (if after Trinity Sunday)

| 1 Samuel 3:1-10, (11-20) | or | Deuteronomy 5:12-15 |
| Psalm 139:1-6, 13-18 | | Psalm 81:1-10 |

2 Corinthians 4:5-12
Mark 2:23–3:6

49

Proper 5 [10]
Sunday between
June 5 and June 11 inclusive
  (if after Trinity Sunday)

      1 Samuel 8:4-11, (12-15), 16-20,   or   Genesis 3:8-15
        (11:14-15)   Psalm 130
      Psalm 138

               2 Corinthians 4:13–5:1
               Mark 3:20-35

Proper 6 [11]
Sunday between
June 12 and June 18 inclusive
  (if after Trinity Sunday)

      1 Samuel 15:34–16:13   or   Ezekiel 17:22-24
      Psalm 20   Psalm 92:1-4, 12-15

           2 Corinthians 5:6-10, (11-13), 14-17
           Mark 4:26-34

Proper 7 [12]
Sunday between
June 19 and June 25 inclusive
  (if after Trinity Sunday)

      1 Samuel 17:(1*a*, 4-11, 19-23),   or   Job 38:1-11
        32-49   Psalm 107:1-3, 23-32
      Psalm 9:9-20
        or
      1 Samuel 17:57–18:5, 10-16
      Psalm 133

               2 Corinthians 6:1-13
               Mark 4:35-41

Proper 8 [13]
Sunday between
June 26 and July 2 inclusive

      2 Samuel 1:1, 17-27   or   Wisdom of Solomon 1:13-15;
      Psalm 130   2:23-24
                                      Lamentations 3:23-33
                                     or Psalm 30

               2 Corinthians 8:7-15
               Mark 5:21-43

Proper 9 [14]
Sunday between
July 3 and July 9 inclusive

    2 Samuel 5:1-5, 9-10   or   Ezekiel 2:1-5
    Psalm 48   Psalm 123

            2 Corinthians 12:2-10
            Mark 6:1-13

Proper 10 [15]
Sunday between
July 10 and July 16 inclusive

    2 Samuel 6:1-5, 12*b*-19   or   Amos 7:7-15
    Psalm 24   Psalm 85:8-13

            Ephesians 1:3-14
            Mark 6:14-29

Proper 11 [16]
Sunday between
July 17 and July 23 inclusive

    2 Samuel 7:1-14*a*   or   Jeremiah 23:1-6
    Psalm 89:20-37   Psalm 23

            Ephesians 2:11-22
            Mark 6:30-34, 53-56

Proper 12 [17]
Sunday between
July 24 and July 30 inclusive

    2 Samuel 11:1-15   or   2 Kings 4:42-44
    Psalm 14   Psalm 145:10-18

            Ephesians 3:14-21
             John 6:1-21

Proper 13 [18]
Sunday between
July 31 and August 6 inclusive

    2 Samuel 11:26–12:13*a*   or   Exodus 16:2-4, 9-15
    Psalm 51:1-12   Psalm 78:23-29

            Ephesians 4:1-16
            John 6:24-35

Proper 14 [19]
Sunday between
August 7 and August 13 inclusive

> 2 Samuel 18:5-9, 15, 31-33 or 1 Kings 19:4-8
> Psalm 130   Psalm 34:1-8
>
>   Ephesians 4:25–5:2
>   John 6:35, 41-51

Proper 15 [20]
Sunday between
August 14 and August 20 inclusive

> 1 Kings 2:10-12; 3:3-14   or Proverbs 9:1-6
> Psalm 111   Psalm 34:9-14
>
>   Ephesians 5:15-20
>   John 6:51-58

Proper 16 [21]
Sunday between
August 21 and August 27 inclusive

> 1 Kings 8:(1, 6, 10-11), 22-30, or Joshua 24:1-2a, 14-18
> 41-43   Psalm 34:15-22
> Psalm 84
>
>   Ephesians 6:10-20
>   John 6:56-69

Proper 17 [22]
Sunday between
August 28 and September 3 inclusive

> Song of Solomon 2:8-13   or Deuteronomy 4:1-2, 6-9
> Psalm 45:1-2, 6-9   Psalm 15
>
>   James 1:17-27
>   Mark 7:1-8, 14-15, 21-23

Proper 18 [23]
Sunday between
September 4 and September 10 inclusive

> Proverbs 22:1-2, 8-9, 22-23 or Isaiah 35:4-7a
> Psalm 125   Psalm 146
>
>   James 2:1-10, (11-13), 14-17
>   Mark 7:24-37

Proper 19 [24]
Sunday between
September 11 and September 17 inclusive

Proverbs 1:20-33   or   Isaiah 50:4-9*a*
Psalm 19   Psalm 116:1-9
  or Wisdom of Solomon 7:26–8:1

James 3:1-12
Mark 8:27-38

Proper 20 [25]
Sunday between
September 18 and September 24 inclusive

Proverbs 31:10-31   or   Wisdom of Solomon 1:16–2:1, 12-22
Psalm 1   or Jeremiah 11:18-20
                                                Psalm 54

James 3:13–4:3, 7-8*a*
Mark 9:30-37

Proper 21 [26]
Sunday between
September 25 and October 1 inclusive

Esther 7:1-6, 9-10; 9:20-22   or   Numbers 11:4-6, 10-16, 24-29
Psalm 124   Psalm 19:7-14

James 5:13-20
Mark 9:38-50

Proper 22 [27]
Sunday between
October 2 and October 8 inclusive

Job 1:1; 2:1-10   or   Genesis 2:18-24
Psalm 26   Psalm 8

Hebrews 1:1-4; 2:5-12
Mark 10:2-16

Proper 23 [28]
Sunday between
October 9 and October 15 inclusive

Job 23:1-9, 16-17   or   Amos 5:6-7, 10-15
Psalm 22:1-15   Psalm 90:12-17

Hebrews 4:12-16
Mark 10:17-31

Proper 24 [29]
Sunday between
October 16 and October 22 inclusive

    Job 38:1-7, (34-41)   or   Isaiah 53:4-12
    Psalm 104:1-9, 24, 35c   Psalm 91:9-16

               Hebrews 5:1-10
               Mark 10:35-45

Proper 25 [30]
Sunday between
October 23 and October 29 inclusive

    Job 42:1-6, 10-17   or   Jeremiah 31:7-9
    Psalm 34:1-8, (19-22)   Psalm 126

               Hebrews 7:23-28
               Mark 10:46-52

Proper 26 [31]
Sunday between
October 30 and November 5 inclusive

    Ruth 1:1-18   or   Deuteronomy 6:1-9
    Psalm 146   Psalm 119:1-8

               Hebrews 9:11-14
               Mark 12:28-34

Proper 27 [32]
Sunday between
November 6 and November 12 inclusive

    Ruth 3:1-5; 4:13-17   or   1 Kings 17:8-16
    Psalm 127   Psalm 146

               Hebrews 9:24-28
               Mark 12:38-44

Proper 28 [33]
Sunday between
November 13 and November 19 inclusive

    1 Samuel 1:4-20   or   Daniel 12:1-3
    1 Samuel 2:1-10   Psalm 16

               Hebrews 10:11-14, (15-18), 19-25
               Mark 13:1-8

Proper 29 [34]
(Reign of Christ or Christ the King)
Sunday between
November 20 and November 26 inclusive

    2 Samuel 23:1-7   or   Daniel 7:9-10, 13-14
    Psalm 132:1-12, (13-18)   Psalm 93

                    Revelation 1:4*b*-8
                    John 18:33-37

All Saints   Wisdom of Solomon 3:1-9
November 1 or the   or Isaiah 25:6-9
First Sunday in November   Psalm 24
                    Revelation 21:1-6*a*
                    John 11:32-44

Thanksgiving Day   Joel 2:21-27
Fourth Thursday in November   Psalm 126
  (U.S.)   1 Timothy 2:1-7
Second Monday in October (Can.)   Matthew 6:25-33

YEAR C

Begins on the First Sunday of Advent in 1994,
1997, 2000, 2003.

SEASON OF ADVENT

First Sunday of Advent

    Jeremiah 33:14-16
Psalm 25:1-10
1 Thessalonians 3:9-13
Luke 21:25-36

Second Sunday of Advent

    Baruch 5:1-9
   or Malachi 3:1-4
Luke 1:68-79
Philippians 1:3-11
Luke 3:1-6

Third Sunday of Advent

    Zephaniah 3:14-20
Isaiah 12:2-6
Philippians 4:4-7
Luke 3:7-18

Fourth Sunday of Advent

    Micah 5:2-5*a*
Luke 1:47-55
   or Psalm 80:1-7
Hebrews 10:5-10
Luke 1:39-45, (46-55)

SEASON OF CHRISTMAS

Nativity of the Lord
  (Christmas Day)

    Any of the following three Propers may be used on Christmas
Eve/Day.

The readings from Propers II and III for Christmas may be used as alternatives for Christmas Day. If Proper III is not used on Christmas Day, it should be used at some service during the Christmas cycle because of the significance of John's prologue.

Christmas, Proper I (A, B, C)	Isaiah 9:2-7 Psalm 96 Titus 2:11-14 Luke 2:1-14, (15-20)
Christmas, Proper II (A, B, C)	Isaiah 62:6-12 Psalm 97 Titus 3:4-7 Luke 2:(1-7), 8-20
Christmas, Proper III (A, B, C)	Isaiah 52:7-10 Psalm 98 Hebrews 1:1-4, (5-12) John 1:1-14

First Sunday after Christmas Day

The following readings are used on the First Sunday after Christmas unless the readings for the Epiphany of the Lord are preferred.

	1 Samuel 2:18-20, 26 Psalm 148 Colossians 3:12-17 Luke 2:41-52
January 1—Holy Name of Jesus (Mary, Mother of God) (A, B, C)	Numbers 6:22-27 Psalm 8 Galatians 4:4-7 or Philippians 2:5-11 Luke 2:15-21
January 1—When observed as New Year's Day (A, B, C)	Ecclesiastes 3:1-13 Psalm 8 Revelation 21:1-6a Matthew 25:31-46

Second Sunday after Christmas Day (A, B, C)

The following readings are provided for use when Epiphany (January 6) is celebrated on a weekday following the Second Sunday after Christmas Day.

Jeremiah 31:7-14
  or Sirach 24:1-12
Psalm 147:12-20
  or Wisdom of Solomon 10:15-21
Ephesians 1:3-14
John 1:(1-9), 10-18

SEASON OF EPIPHANY (ORDINARY TIME)

Epiphany of the Lord (A, B, C)

Isaiah 60:1-6
Psalm 72:1-7, 10-14
Ephesians 3:1-12
Matthew 2:1-12

Baptism of the Lord [1]
  (First Sunday after the Epiphany)

Isaiah 43:1-7
Psalm 29
Acts 8:14-17
Luke 3:15-17, 21-22

Second Sunday after the Epiphany [2]

Isaiah 62:1-5
Psalm 36:5-10
1 Corinthians 12:1-11
John 2:1-11

Third Sunday after the Epiphany [3]

Nehemiah 8:1-3, 5-6, 8-10
Psalm 19
1 Corinthians 12:12-31a
Luke 4:14-21

Fourth Sunday after the Epiphany [4]

Jeremiah 1:4-10
Psalm 71:1-6
1 Corinthians 13:1-13
Luke 4:21-30

Fifth Sunday after the Epiphany [5]

Isaiah 6:1-8, (9-13)
Psalm 138
1 Corinthians 15:1-11
Luke 5:1-11

Sixth Sunday after the Epiphany [6]

> *Proper 1.* If this is the Sunday before Ash Wednesday, this Proper
> may be replaced, in those Churches using Transfiguration readings
> on this day, by the readings for the Last Sunday after the Epiphany.

Jeremiah 17:5-10
Psalm 1
1 Corinthians 15:12-20
Luke 6:17-26

Seventh Sunday after the Epiphany [7]

Proper 2. If this is the Sunday before Ash Wednesday, this Proper may be replaced, in those Churches using Transfiguration readings on this day, by the readings for the Last Sunday after the Epiphany.

Genesis 45:3-11, 15
Psalm 37:1-11, 39-40
1 Corinthians 15:35-38, 42-50
Luke 6:27-38

Eighth Sunday after the Epiphany [8]

Proper 3. If this is the Sunday before Ash Wednesday, this Proper may be replaced, in those Churches using Transfiguration readings on this day, by the readings for the Last Sunday after the Epiphany.

Sirach 27:4-7
   or Isaiah 55:10-13
Psalm 92:1-4, 12-15
1 Corinthians 15:51-58
Luke 6:39-49

Ninth Sunday after the Epiphany [9]

Proper 4. The following readings are for Churches whose calendar requires this Sunday, and do not observe the Last Sunday after the Epiphany as Transfiguration.

1 Kings 8:22-23, 41-43
Psalm 96:1-9
Galatians 1:1-12
Luke 7:1-10

Last Sunday after the Epiphany
(Transfiguration Sunday)

The following readings are used in Churches where the Last Sunday after the Epiphany is observed as Transfiguration Sunday.

Exodus 34:29-35
Psalm 99
2 Corinthians 3:12–4:2
Luke 9:28-36, (37-43)

SEASON OF LENT

Ash Wednesday (A, B, C)	Joel 2:1-2, 12-17 or Isaiah 58:1-12 Psalm 51:1-17 2 Corinthians 5:20*b*–6:10 Matthew 6:1-6, 16-21
First Sunday in Lent	Deuteronomy 26:1-11 Psalm 91:1-2, 9-16 Romans 10:8*b*-13 Luke 4:1-13
Second Sunday in Lent	Genesis 15:1-12, 17-18 Psalm 27 Philippians 3:17–4:1 Luke 13:31-35 or Luke 9:28-36
Third Sunday in Lent	Isaiah 55:1-9 Psalm 63:1-8 1 Corinthians 10:1-13 Luke 13:1-9
Fourth Sunday in Lent	Joshua 5:9-12 Psalm 32 2 Corinthians 5:16-21 Luke 15:1-3, 11*b*-32
Fifth Sunday in Lent	Isaiah 43:16-21 Psalm 126 Philippians 3:4*b*-14 John 12:1-8

Sixth Sunday in Lent
(Passion Sunday or Palm Sunday)

> Those who do not observe the procession with palms and do not wish to use the passion gospel may substitute the gospel and psalm given for the Liturgy of the Passion with the gospel and psalm indicated for the Liturgy of the Palms. Whenever possible, the whole passion narrative should be read.

Liturgy of the Palms	Luke 19:28-40 Psalm 118:1-2, 19-29

Liturgy of the Passion

Isaiah 50:4-9*a*
Psalm 31:9-16
Philippians 2:5-11
Luke 22:14–23:56
    or Luke 23:1-49

HOLY WEEK

Monday of Holy Week (A, B, C)

Isaiah 42:1-9
Psalm 36:5-11
Hebrews 9:11-15
John 12:1-11

Tuesday of Holy Week (A, B, C)

Isaiah 49:1-7
Psalm 71:1-14
1 Corinthians 1:18-31
John 12:20-36

Wednesday of Holy Week (A, B, C)

Isaiah 50:4-9*a*
Psalm 70
Hebrews 12:1-3
John 13:21-32

Holy Thursday (A, B, C)

Exodus 12:1-4, (5-10), 11-14
Psalm 116:1-2, 12-19
1 Corinthians 11:23-26
John 13:1-17, 31*b*-35

Good Friday (A, B, C)

Isaiah 52:13–53:12
Psalm 22
Hebrews 10:16-25
    or Hebrews 4:14-16; 5:7-9
John 18:1–19:42

Holy Saturday (A, B, C)

The following readings are for use at services other than the Easter Vigil.

Job 14:1-14
    or Lamentations 3:1-9, 19-24
Psalm 31:1-4, 15-16
1 Peter 4:1-8
Matthew 27:57-66
    or John 19:38-42

SEASON OF EASTER

Resurrection of the Lord
Easter Vigil (A, B, C)

> The following readings and psalms are provided for use at the Easter Vigil. A minimum of three Old Testament readings should be chosen. The reading from Exodus 14 should always be used.

Old Testament Readings
and Psalms (A, B, C):

	Genesis 1:1–2:4a
	Psalm 136:1-9, 23-26
	Genesis 7:1-5, 11-18; 8:6-18; 9:8-13
	Psalm 46
	Genesis 22:1-18
	Psalm 16
	Exodus 14:10-31; 15:20-21
	Exodus 15:1b-13, 17-18
	Isaiah 55:1-11
	Isaiah 12:2-6
	Baruch 3:9-15, 32–4:4
	or Proverbs 8:1-8, 19-21; 9:4b-6
	Psalm 19
	Ezekiel 36:24-28
	Psalm 42 and 43
	Ezekiel 37:1-14
	Psalm 143
	Zephaniah 3:14-20
	Psalm 98

New Testament Reading (A, B, C):   Romans 6:3-11
Psalm 114

Gospel: Luke 24:1-12

Resurrection of the Lord
Easter Day

First Reading: Acts 10:34-43
or Isaiah 65:17-25
Psalm 118:1-2, 14-24

Second Reading: 1 Corinthians 15:19-26
or Acts 10:34-43

Gospel: John 20:1-18
or Luke 24:1-12

Easter Evening (A, B, C)

> The following readings are for occasions when the main (eucharistic) Easter service must be late in the day. They are not intended for Vespers (Evening Prayer) on Easter Evening.

Isaiah 25:6-9
Psalm 114
1 Corinthians 5:6b-8
Luke 24:13-49

Second Sunday of Easter

Acts 5:27-32
Psalm 118:14-29
  or Psalm 150
Revelation 1:4-8
John 20:19-31

Third Sunday of Easter

Acts 9:1-6, (7-20)
Psalm 30
Revelation 5:11-14
John 21:1-19

Fourth Sunday of Easter

Acts 9:36-43
Psalm 23
Revelation 7:9-17
John 10:22-30

Fifth Sunday of Easter

Acts 11:1-18
Psalm 148
Revelation 21:1-6
John 13:31-35

Sixth Sunday of Easter

Acts 16:9-15
Psalm 67
Revelation 21:10, 22–22:5
John 14:23-29
  or John 5:1-9

Ascension of the Lord (A, B, C)

> These readings may also be used on the Seventh Sunday of Easter.

Acts 1:1-11
Psalm 47
  or Psalm 110
Ephesians 1:15-23
Luke 24:44-53

Seventh Sunday of Easter   Acts 16:16-34
                                            Psalm 97
                                            Revelation 22:12-14, 16-17, 20-21
                                            John 17:20-26

Day of Pentecost

   If the passage from Genesis is chosen for the First Reading, the
   passage from Acts is used as the Second Reading.

   First Reading: Acts 2:1-21
                                               or Genesis 11:1-9
                                            Psalm 104:24-34, 35b

   Second Reading: Romans 8:14-17
                                               or Acts 2:1-21

   Gospel: John 14:8-17, (25-27)

SEASON AFTER PENTECOST (ORDINARY TIME)

Trinity Sunday   Proverbs 8:1-4, 22-31
   (First Sunday after Pentecost)   Psalm 8
                                            Romans 5:1-5
                                            John 16:12-15

   If the Sunday between May 24 and 28 inclusive follows Trinity
   Sunday, Proper for Eighth Sunday after the Epiphany [8] is used.

Proper 4 [9]
Sunday between
May 29 and June 4 inclusive
   (if after Trinity Sunday)

      1 Kings 18:20-21, (22-29), 30-39   or 1 Kings 8:22-23, 41-43
      Psalm 96   Psalm 96:1-9

                     Galatians 1:1-12
                     Luke 7:1-10

Proper 5 [10]
Sunday between
June 5 and June 11 inclusive
   (if after Trinity Sunday)

      1 Kings 17:8-16, (17-24)   or 1 Kings 17:17-24
      Psalm 146   Psalm 30

                     Galatians 1:11-24
                     Luke 7:11-17

Proper 6 [11]
Sunday between
June 12 and June 18 inclusive
  (if after Trinity Sunday)

  1 Kings 21:1-10, (11-14), 15-21*a* or 2 Samuel 11:26–12:10, 13-15
  Psalm 5:1-8   Psalm 32

        Galatians 2:15-21
        Luke 7:36–8:3

Proper 7 [12]
Sunday between
June 19 and June 25 inclusive
  (if after Trinity Sunday)

  1 Kings 19:1-4, (5-7), 8-15*a* or Isaiah 65:1-9
  Psalm 42 and 43   Psalm 22:19-28

        Galatians 3:23-29
        Luke 8:26-39

Proper 8 [13]
Sunday between
June 26 and July 2 inclusive

  2 Kings 2:1-2, 6-14   or 1 Kings 19:15-16, 19-21
  Psalm 77:1-2, 11-20   Psalm 16

        Galatians 5:1, 13-25
        Luke 9:51-62

Proper 9 [14]
Sunday between
July 3 and July 9 inclusive

  2 Kings 5:1-14   or Isaiah 66:10-14
  Psalm 30   Psalm 66:1-9

        Galatians 6:(1-6), 7-16
        Luke 10:1-11, 16-20

Proper 10 [15]
Sunday between
July 10 and July 16 inclusive

  Amos 7:7-17   or Deuteronomy 30:9-14
  Psalm 82   Psalm 25:1-10

        Colossians 1:1-14
        Luke 10:25-37

Proper 11 [16]
Sunday between
July 17 and July 23 inclusive

> Amos 8:1-12 or Genesis 18:1-10*a*
> Psalm 52 Psalm 15
>
> Colossians 1:15-28
> Luke 10:38-42

Proper 12 [17]
Sunday between
July 24 and July 30 inclusive

> Hosea 1:2-10 or Genesis 18:20-32
> Psalm 85 Psalm 138
>
> Colossians 2:6-15, (16-19)
> Luke 11:1-13

Proper 13 [18]
Sunday between
July 31 and August 6 inclusive

> Hosea 11:1-11 or Ecclesiastes 1:2, 12-14; 2:18-23
> Psalm 107:1-9, 43 Psalm 49:1-12
>
> Colossians 3:1-11
> Luke 12:13-21

Proper 14 [19]
Sunday between
August 7 and August 13 inclusive

> Isaiah 1:1, 10-20 or Genesis 15:1-6
> Psalm 50:1-8, 22-23 Psalm 33:12-22
>
> Hebrews 11:1-3, 8-16
> Luke 12:32-40

Proper 15 [20]
Sunday between
August 14 and August 20 inclusive

> Isaiah 5:1-7 or Jeremiah 23:23-29
> Psalm 80:1-2, 8-19 Psalm 82
>
> Hebrews 11:29–12:2
> Luke 12:49-56

Proper 16 [21]
Sunday between
August 21 and August 27 inclusive

    Jeremiah 1:4-10   or Isaiah 58:9*b*-14
    Psalm 71:1-6   Psalm 103:1-8

           Hebrews 12:18-29
           Luke 13:10-17

Proper 17 [22]
Sunday between
August 28 and September 3 inclusive

    Jeremiah 2:4-13   or Sirach 10:12-18
    Psalm 81:1, 10-16   or Proverbs 25:6-7
                    Psalm 112

           Hebrews 13:1-8, 15-16
           Luke 14:1, 7-14

Proper 18 [23]
Sunday between
September 4 and September 10 inclusive

    Jeremiah 18:1-11   or Deuteronomy 30:15-20
    Psalm 139:1-6, 13-18   Psalm 1

           Philemon 1-21
           Luke 14:25-33

Proper 19 [24]
Sunday between
September 11 and September 17 inclusive

    Jeremiah 4:11-12, 22-28   or Exodus 32:7-14
    Psalm 14   Psalm 51:1-10

           1 Timothy 1:12-17
           Luke 15:1-10

Proper 20 [25]
Sunday between
September 18 and September 24 inclusive

    Jeremiah 8:18–9:1   or Amos 8:4-7
    Psalm 79:1-9   Psalm 113

           1 Timothy 2:1-7
           Luke 16:1-13

Proper 21 [26]
Sunday between
September 25 and October 1 inclusive

Jeremiah 32:1-3a, 6-15   or Amos 6:1a, 4-7
Psalm 91:1-6, 14-16   Psalm 146

                          1 Timothy 6:6-19
                          Luke 16:19-31

Proper 22 [27]
Sunday between
October 2 and October 8 inclusive

Lamentations 1:1-6   or Habakkuk 1:1-4; 2:1-4
Lamentations 3:19-26   Psalm 37:1-9
    or Psalm 137

                          2 Timothy 1:1-14
                          Luke 17:5-10

Proper 23 [28]
Sunday between
October 9 and October 15 inclusive

Jeremiah 29:1, 4-7   or 2 Kings 5:1-3, 7-15c
Psalm 66:1-12   Psalm 111

                          2 Timothy 2:8-15
                          Luke 17:11-19

Proper 24 [29]
Sunday between
October 16 and October 22 inclusive

Jeremiah 31:27-34   or Genesis 32:22-31
Psalm 119:97-104   Psalm 121

                          2 Timothy 3:14–4:5
                          Luke 18:1-8

Proper 25 [30]
Sunday between
October 23 and October 29 inclusive

Joel 2:23-32   or Sirach 35:12-17
Psalm 65   or Jeremiah 14:7-10, 19-22
                                              Psalm 84:1-7

                          2 Timothy 4:6-8, 16-18
                          Luke 18:9-14

Proper 26 [31]
Sunday between
October 30 and November 5 inclusive

    Habakkuk 1:1-4; 2:1-4   or Isaiah 1:10-18
    Psalm 119:137-144   Psalm 32:1-7

             2 Thessalonians 1:1-4, 11-12
             Luke 19:1-10

Proper 27 [32]
Sunday between
November 6 and November 12 inclusive

    Haggai 1:15*b*–2:9   or Job 19:23-27*a*
    Psalm 145:1-5, 17-21   Psalm 17:1-9
      or Psalm 98

             2 Thessalonians 2:1-5, 13-17
             Luke 20:27-38

Proper 28 [33]
Sunday between
November 13 and November 19 inclusive

    Isaiah 65:17-25   or Malachi 4:1-2*a*
    Isaiah 12   Psalm 98

             2 Thessalonians 3:6-13
             Luke 21:5-19

Proper 29 [34]
(Reign of Christ or Christ the King)
Sunday between
November 20 and November 26 inclusive

    Jeremiah 23:1-6   or Jeremiah 23:1-6
    Luke 1:68-79   Psalm 46

             Colossians 1:11-20
             Luke 23:33-43

All Saints
November 1 or the
First Sunday in November

Daniel 7:1-3, 15-18
Psalm 149
Ephesians 1:11-23
Luke 6:20-31

Thanksgiving Day
Fourth Thursday in November
  (U.S.)
Second Monday in October (Can.)

Deuteronomy 26:1-11
Psalm 100
Philippians 4:4-9
John 6:25-35

SPECIAL DAYS

(A, B, C)

February 2
Presentation of the Lord (A, B, C)

    Malachi 3:1-4
    Psalm 84
      or Psalm 24:7-10
    Hebrews 2:14-18
    Luke 2:22-40

March 25
Annunciation of the Lord (A, B, C)

    Isaiah 7:10-14
    Psalm 45
      or Psalm 40:5-10
    Hebrews 10:4-10
    Luke 1:26-38

May 31
Visitation of Mary to Elizabeth (A, B, C)

    1 Samuel 2:1-10
    Psalm 113
    Romans 12:9-16*b*
    Luke 1:39-57

September 14
Holy Cross (A, B, C)

    Numbers 21:4*b*-9
    Psalm 98:1-5
      or Psalm 78:1-2, 34-38
    1 Corinthians 1:18-24
    John 3:13-17

THE STORY OF THE
COMMON LECTIONARY

I. The 1969 Lectionary and Other Lectionaries

In 1963, the Second Vatican Council called the Roman Catholic Church to promote a "warm and living love of Scripture" among its members. A greater number and a wider variety of Scripture texts were to be read during the liturgy, and preaching was to be more scriptural. The teaching of the word of God was seen as the primary duty of the clergy. In response to these decisions, the Catholic Church produced in 1969, after several years of international consultations, an extensive table of readings for many celebrations: Sunday, weekdays, feast days, sacraments, other rites of the Church, and other occasions. On each Lord's Day, there are three readings: the first one is usually from the Old Testament, the second from the epistles, and the third from one of the gospels. After the first reading, a brief excerpt from a psalm is sung or prayed as a response to the proclamation.

In many countries, the selected passages are printed in a special book, called a lectionary or book of readings. The table of readings issued in 1969 is now used in the Roman Catholic Church throughout the world in some 400 languages. A fuller introduction and a few additional texts were added to the lectionary in 1981.

Other lectionaries

Within less than a year of the issuing of the Roman lectionary for Mass in 1969, the value of this table of Sunday readings was recognized by other churches in the United States and Canada. The process of appropriation began with the publication in 1970 of *The Worshipbook-Services*, a service book jointly produced by three Presbyterian churches in the United States. Soon after, the Episcopal and Lutheran Churches in the United States included the table of readings in preliminary studies, which led to its inclusion in the *Book of Common Prayer* and the *Lutheran Book of Worship*. The Disciples of Christ and the United Church of Christ in the U.S.A. adopted the Presbyterian version for voluntary use.

The proliferation of versions of the original Roman table of Sunday readings was both ecumenically encouraging and also dismaying. Each of the five versions differed slightly from the others. Attempts by local clergy to meet for sermon planning were hampered by the different texts and arrangements, and published materials were confronted by multiple options. There was an increasing demand for some standardization.

In 1974, the Consultation on Church Union (COCU) published a consensus edition in pamphlet form. At that time, COCU represented nine Protestant denominations in the United States.

Developing a common ecumenical lectionary

Early in 1978, in Washington, DC, at a meeting sponsored by the Consultation on Common Texts, it was agreed that consensus was needed on the list of Sunday readings. Furthermore, they felt that there was a need to revise the manner in which the Old Testament readings were chosen in the Roman lectionary in order to provide a more representative presentation of the Jewish Scriptures. It was also suggested that in some cases the Old Testament reading be aligned with the epistle reading.

The Consultation on Common Texts set up a working group, the North American Committee on Calendar and Lectionary, composed of pastors and scholars from the Roman Catholic, Episcopal, Presbyterian, Lutheran, and United Methodist churches. The working principles of this group were described in this way:

a. The basic calendar and structure of three readings presupposed by the Roman lectionary are assumed.

b. The gospel pericopes (readings) are assumed with only minor textual rearrangement to accommodate churches which use a Bible for liturgical use rather than a lectionary.

c. The New Testament pericopes are largely accepted with some lengthening of pericopes and minor textual rearrangement to include textual material such as apostolic and personal greetings and local ecclesial issues.

d. The typological choice of Old Testament pericopes has been addressed in that this has been the area of most serious criticism from Catholic and Protestant scholars and pastors. In response, the committee has proposed a revision of the Roman table for a number of Sundays of the year (Ordinary Time) in each of the three cycles. The lessons are still typologically controlled by the gospel, but in a broader way than Sunday by Sunday, in order to make possible semicontinuous reading of some significant Old Testament narratives.

The finished work of this committee was published in 1983 as the Consultation's proposal to the churches of North America. This book, entitled *Common Lectionary* (New York: The Church Hymnal Corporation, 1983), contained an introduction, the tables of readings, some explanation of the specific choices, and showed how it had moved toward a consensus among the variety of versions published in the 1970s.

II. Critiques of the 1983 Lectionary

It was always understood by the CCT that the 1983 table of readings was for experimental use, and criticisms were invited. After two three-year cycles of testing, the CCT appointed a task force to examine the tables, to listen to critiques from many levels and many groups, and to take them into account. Hundreds of individuals and dozens of churches submitted helpful criticisms. All of these have been carefully noted, evaluated, and considered by the task force in its process of revision.

The critiques received were generally in one of five different areas: a) the use of Scripture; b) the place of women in the lectionary; c) problems of the common calendar; d) the need for a cycle of first readings more directly linked to the gospel of the day in the Sundays after Pentecost; e) and sensitivity to the way some Scripture texts are heard by Christian congregations today.

Use of Scripture

Many people asked whether the canon of Scripture had been given appropriate treatment in *Common Lectionary* (1983). For example, much criticism was received of the handling of the Old Testament prophets.

In the revision, the task force examined the whole of the prophetic message, and as a result, in place of the canonical order of the prophets (followed essentially in year C), presented the prophets chronologically in the Sundays after Pentecost. The ministry of Elijah and Elisha as recounted in the books of Kings is given less space, while the ministry and teaching of Jeremiah has become central to the cycle.

Among the important critiques of the use of Scripture was that of the Episcopal Church. The concern of that church was to reconcile the slight differences in the current Old Testament readings among the Episcopal, Lutheran, and Roman Catholic churches. The critique did not approve of the treatment of the Old Testament in the 1983 edition of the *Common Lectionary*. It spoke of: 1) the notion of relating the Old Testament and gospel as proclaiming the paschal mystery on the Lord's Day; 2) the pastoral confusion caused to congregations in our churches by three unrelated readings; 3) and the pastoral problems of three lengthy readings and a psalm in churches where all are read. Some Lutherans and Roman Catholics also identified with this critique.

The use of the psalter was also frequently criticized. In its revision, the task force affirmed that the psalm (or a scriptural canticle) should be chosen as the liturgical response to the first reading, and that it should fit harmoniously within the general tenor of the celebration. In selecting the psalms, the task force sought to respect the breadth and diversity of the psalter, and to use some scriptural canticles where appropriate. The more familiar psalms are repeated occasionally. An attempt was made to respect the integrity of the content of the psalm itself; where length precluded the use of the whole, the selection of verses seeks to reflect the movement of the psalm. On occasion a possible fuller reading of the psalm is indicated through the use of brackets. In the *Revised Common Lectionary*, 105 psalms and ten canticles are included.

The publication in 1990 of the *New Revised Standard Version* (NRSV) by the National Council of Churches of Christ in the USA made it necessary to examine the versification of all the readings in the *Common Lectionary*. For example, the song of Mary (Magnificat) in the *Revised Standard Version* began at Luke 1:46*b*. In the NRSV it begins at 1:47.

Some criticism was made of the beginning and ending of specific readings in the 1983 *Common Lectionary*. As a result, the task force looked carefully at all readings in the light of the NRSV, and made numerous minor adjustments. For example, the 1983 edition gave Philippians 2:9-13 as the versification of the ancient kenotic hymn, while the present edition gives 2:5-11 as the more appropriate versification.

Place of women in the lectionary

A major critique of the 1983 lectionary by many men and women concerned the place of women in the readings. The task force recognized the significant, if often overlooked, role played by women in the biblical story. As a consequence the *Revised Common Lectionary* has added a number of readings which make this more evident: for example, the promise of God to Sarah for her faithfulness, the contribution of the Hebrew midwives to the saving of the children of the Hebrew slaves in Egypt, the encounter of the Syro-Phoenician woman with Jesus, and the apostolic ministry of Lydia.

A number of omissions were drawn to the attention of the CCT. The task force examined these and searched for others. For example, the story of Hagar and her infant, Ishmael (Genesis 21:8-21), is included in year A.

Problems of the common calendar

A number of minor issues surfaced with regard to the calendar. The 1992 lectionary has recognized the need to add readings for a Ninth Sunday after Epiphany, as well as for Holy Saturday.

First reading more closely linked to gospel

A number of respondents to the 1983 edition were concerned to develop more fully the reading of the Old Testament Scriptures in relation to the gospel, as already noted.

Sensitivity to Scripture passages

Both users and students of the 1983 lectionary have made the observation that problems are sometimes created because Scripture texts, when taken out of their cultural and religious context in the Ancient Near East, may be misunderstood by late twentieth century congregations. In particular, the *Revised Common Lectionary* has paid attention to the tragic history of the abuse of biblical materials to support

Christian anti-Semitism. The need to avoid such abuse is one of the basic principles of this lectionary.

III. Worldwide Interest in Lectionary Renewal

In 1967, the Joint Liturgical Group in Great Britain developed a two-year thematic lectionary, which has been widely adopted. In 1990, they produced *A Four Year Lectionary*, which is an exploration of the possibility of having a year of John as well as the three synoptic years. In this lectionary, rather than having a theme, the readings are said to be merely "linked."

The English Language Liturgical Consultation (ELLC) has endorsed the *Common Lectionary* as the most promising version of an international ecumenical lectionary. Representatives of ELLC have worked as members of the task force preparing this *Revised Common Lectionary*. ELLC includes ecumenical associations of Churches from Australia, Canada, England, New Zealand, Scotland, South Africa, the United States, and Wales.

Worldwide groupings of various denominations which represent several language groups have also begun to show interest in lectionary renewal. There is known to be considerable interest in and use of the *Common Lectionary* among Methodists and Presbyterians in Korea. In 1989, the ELLC asked the World Council of Churches and the Pontifical Council for Promoting Christian Unity to consider becoming involved in a worldwide, multinational, and ecumenical dialogue on lectionary renewal and reform, based on the original concept presented in the Roman *Lectionary for Mass* of 1969, as modified in the *Common Lectionary*.

MEMBERS OF THE TASK FORCE ON THE REVISED COMMON LECTIONARY

The task force that prepared the *Revised Common Lectionary* was appointed by the Consultation on Common Texts in November of 1986. The membership has involved persons whose Churches and liturgical conferences actively use the *Common Lectionary*, have tested the *Common Lectionary*, or have a serious interest in adopting the *Revised Common Lectionary* for use. The members of the task force included:

The Reverend Dr. Neil Alexander, Professor of Worship at General Seminary in New York City, representative of the Lutheran Churches from 1986–1987.

The Reverend Dr. Horace T. Allen, Jr., Professor of Worship and Preaching at Boston University School of Theology, representative of the English Language Liturgical Consultation, member of the committee that created the 1983 Common Lectionary, and representative of The Presbyterian Church (USA).

The Reverend Robert J. Brooks, The Presiding Bishop's Staff Officer of The Episcopal Church: Washington Office, member of the Standing Liturgical Commission (1985–1988), and representative of The Episcopal Church.

The Reverend Dr. Thomas D. Dipko, Bishop of the Ohio Area of the United Church of Christ, and representative of The United Church of Christ.

The Reverend John Fitzsimmons, Chairperson of the Advisory Committee of the International Commission on English in the Liturgy (ICEL), Roman Catholic, and representative of the English Language Liturgical Consultation (ELLC), beginning in 1990.

The Reverend Paul Gibson, Liturgical Officer of the Anglican Church of Canada, chair of the Consultation on Common Texts from 1986–1989, and representative of the Anglican Church of Canda.

Dr. Fred Graham, Consultant on Congregational Worship and representative of The United Church of Canada, beginning in 1988.

The Reverend Canon Dr. Donald Gray, Canon of Westminster, Church of England, Chairman of the Joint Liturgical Group (JLG) of Great Britain, and representative of the English Language Liturgical Consultation (ELLC).

The Reverend Dr. Gerald Hobbs, Professor of Church History, Vancouver School of Theology, Vancouver, British Columbia, The United Church of Canada, Standing Consultant with particular focus on the psalms, beginning in 1989.

The Reverend Canon Dr. David R. Holeton, Professor in Divinity at Trinity College, Toronto, and representative of the Anglican Church of Canada.

The Reverend Thomas A. Langford, III, Assistant General Secretary of The Section on Worship of The United Methodist Church, chair of the Task Force on the *Revised Common Lectionary,* and representative of The United Methodist Church.

The Reverend Edward Matthews, past Secretary of Liturgy Office of the Bishops' Conference of England and Wales, Roman Catholic, member of the Joint Liturgical Group (JLG) of Great Britain, member of the Advisory Committee of the International Commission on English in the Liturgy (ICEL), and representative of the English Language Liturgical Consultation (ELLC), 1988–1989.

The Reverend Dr. Fred McNally, Consultant on Congregational Worship and representative of The United Church of Canada, 1988–1989.

Dr. Gail Ramshaw, Professor of Religion at LaSalle University, and representative of the Evangelical Lutheran Church in America, 1987–1992.

HELPFUL READING

Allen, Horace T. "Introduction." In *Common Lectionary: The Lectionary Proposed by the Consultation on Common Texts*. New York: Church Hymnal Corporation, 1983.

————. "Emerging Ecumenical Issues in Worship." *Word and World* 9, no. 1 (Winter 1989):16-22.

————. "The Ecumenical Import of Lectionary Reform." In *Shaping English Liturgy: Studies in Honor of Archbishop Denis Hurley*, 361-384. Edited by Peter C. Finn and James M. Schellman. Washington, DC: Pastoral Press, 1990.

————. "Common Lectionary: Origins, Assumptions, and Issues." *Studia Liturgica* 21, no. 1 (1991):14-30.

Boehringer, Hans. "The Common Lectionary." *Word and World* 10, no. 1 (Winter 1990):27-32.

Bradshaw, Paul. "The Use of the Bible in the Liturgy." *Studia Liturgica* 22 (1992):35-52.

Common Lectionary: The Lectionary Proposed by the Consultation on Common Texts. New York: Church Hymnal Corporation, 1983.

Dudley, Martin. "The Lectionary." In *Towards Liturgy 2000: Preparing for the Revision of the Alternative Service Book*. Edited by Michael Perham, 35-42. London: SPCK/Alcuin Club, 1989.

Gray, Donald, ed. *The Word in Season, Essays by members of the Joint Liturgical Group on the Use of the Bible in Liturgy*. Norwich, England: The Canterbury Press, 1988.

————. "Towards an Ecumenical Eucharistic Lectionary." *Liturgy* 12, no. 4 (1988):149-154.

————. "The Contribution of the Joint Liturgical Group to the Search for an Ecumenical Lectionary." *Studia Liturgica* 21, no. 1 (1991): 31-36.

Heuser, Rick. "Case for a Study of Old Testament Lectionary Texts: Connections Between Ancient Hebrew History and Current Political Affairs in the Middle East."

An unpublished paper by members of the Boston Presbytery of The Presbyterian Church (USA), 1989.

Joint Liturgical Group. *A Four Year Lectionary*. Norwich, England: The Canterbury Press, 1990.

Lengeling, E. J. "Pericopes." In *New Catholic Encyclopedia* 11. New York: McGraw-Hill Book Co., 1967.

Lowry, Eugene L. *Living with the Lectionary: Preaching the Revised Common Lectionary*. Nashville: Abingdon Press, 1992.

Proctor-Smith, Marjorie. "Images of Women in the Lectionary." In *Women—Invisible in Theology and Church*. Edited by Elisabeth Schussler Fiorenza and Mary Collins, 51-62. Edinburgh: T. and T. Clark, 1985.

————. "Reorganizing Victimization: The Intersection between Liturgy and Domestic Violence." *Perkins Journal* (October 1987): 17-27.

Reumann, John. "A History of Lectionaries: From the Synagogue at Nazareth to Post-Vatican II." *Interpretation: A Journal of Bible and Theology* 3, no. 2 (April 1977).

Schuller, Eileen. "Some Criteria for the Choice of Scripture Texts in the Roman Lectionary." In *Shaping English Liturgy: Studies in Honor of Archbishop Denis Hurley*, 385-404. Edited by Peter C. Finn and James M. Schellman. Washington, DC: Pastoral Press, 1990.

Skudlarek, William. "The Structure and Use of the Lectionary" and "The Pastoral Use of the Lectionary." In *The Word in Worship: Preaching in a Liturgical Context*, 31-64. Nashville: Abingdon Press, 1981.

Sloyan, Gerard. "Some Suggestions for a Biblical Three-Year Lectionary." *Worship* 63, no. 6 (November 1989): 521-535.

"Sunday Lectionary Systems." A series of essays in *Studia Liturgica* 21, no. 1 (1991).

INDEX I

Scripture Readings Listed
According to the
Sundays of the Liturgical Year

Is 2:1-5	Advent 1	A		Is 62:6-12	Christmas Day 2	A
Ps 122	Advent 1	A		Ps 97	Christmas Day 2	A
Rom 13:11-14	Advent 1	A		Ti 3:4-7	Christmas Day 2	A
Mt 24:36-44	Advent 1	A		Lk 2:(1-7), 8-20	Christmas Day 2	A
Is 11:1-10	Advent 2	A				
Ps 72:1-7, 18-19	Advent 2	A		Is 52:7-10	Christmas Day 3	A
				Ps 98	Christmas Day 3	A
Rom 15:4-13	Advent 2	A		Heb 1:1-4, (5-12)	Christmas Day 3	A
Mt 3:1-12	Advent 2	A		Jn 1:1-14	Christmas Day 3	A
Is 35:1-10	Advent 3	A				
Ps 146:5-10 (Alt)	Advent 3	A		Is 63:7-9	Christmas 1	A
Luke 1:47-55 (Alt resp)	Advent 3	A		Ps 148	Christmas 1	A
				Heb 2:10-18	Christmas 1	A
Jas 5:7-10	Advent 3	A		Mt 2:13-23	Christmas 1	A
Mt 11:2-11	Advent 3	A				
				Nm 6:22-27	Holy Name	A
Is 7:10-16	Advent 4	A		Ps 8	Holy Name	A
Ps 80:1-7, 17-19	Advent 4	A		Gal 4:4-7 (Alt)	Holy Name	A
				Phil 2:5-11 (Alt)	Holy Name	A
Rom 1:1-7	Advent 4	A				
Mt 1:18-25	Advent 4	A		Lk 2:15-21	Holy Name	A
Is 9:2-7	Christmas Day 1	A				
Ps 96	Christmas Day 1	A		Eccl 3:1-13	New Year	A
Ti 2:11-14	Christmas Day 1	A		Ps 8	New Year	A
Lk 2:1-14, (15-20)	Christmas Day 1	A		Rv 21:1-6a	New Year	A
				Mt 25:31-46	New Year	A

Mt 28:1-10 (Alt)	Easter	A	Acts 1:1-11	Ascension	A
			Ps 47	Ascension	A
			Eph 1:15-23	Ascension	A
			Lk 24:44-53	Ascension	A
Is 25:6-9	Easter Evening	A			
Ps 114	Easter Evening	A			
1 Cor 5:6b-8	Easter Evening	A	Acts 1:6-14	Easter 7	A
Lk 24:13-49	Easter Evening	A	Ps 68:1-10, 32-35	Easter 7	A
			1 Pt 4:12-14; 5:6-11	Easter 7	A
Acts 2:14a, 22-32	Easter 2	A	Jn 17:1-11	Easter 7	A
Ps 16	Easter 2	A			
1 Pt 1:3-9	Easter 2	A	Acts 2:1-21 (Alt)	Pentecost	A
Jn 20:19-31	Easter 2	A	Nm 11:24-30 (Alt)	Pentecost	A
			Ps 104:24-34, 35b	Pentecost	A
Acts 2:14a, 36-41	Easter 3	A	1 Cor 12:3b-13 (Alt)	Pentecost	A
Ps 116:1-4, 12-19	Easter 3	A	Acts 2:1-21 (Alt)	Pentecost	A
1 Pt 1:17-23	Easter 3	A	Jn 20:19-23 (Alt)	Pentecost	A
Lk 24:13-35	Easter 3	A	Jn 7:37-39 (Alt)	Pentecost	A
Acts 2:42-47	Easter 4	A			
Ps 23	Easter 4	A			
1 Pt 2:19-25	Easter 4	A			
Jn 10:1-10	Easter 4	A	Gn 1:1–2:4a	Trinity Sunday	A
			Ps 8	Trinity Sunday	A
			2 Cor 13:11-13	Trinity Sunday	A
Acts 7:55-60	Easter 5	A	Mt 28:16-20	Trinity Sunday	A
Ps 31:1-5, 15-16	Easter 5	A			
1 Pt 2:2-10	Easter 5	A			
Jn 14:1-14	Easter 5	A			

The Old Testament readings for Proper 4 through Proper 29 (which follow here) provide a pattern of semicontinuous Old Testament readings. If a pattern of paired readings is preferred, in which the Old Testament and gospel readings are closely related, see

Acts 17:22-31	Easter 6	A
Ps 66:8-20	Easter 6	A
1 Pt 3:13-22	Easter 6	A
Jn 14:15-21	Easter 6	A

pp. 92-94. Since each pattern has its own consistency, it is important to select one or the other for use throughout the Sundays that follow Pentecost. For a discussion of these two approaches, see pp. 11 and 16-18 in the introduction.

Gn 6:9-22; 7:24; 8:14-19	Proper 4 [9]	A
Ps 46	Proper 4 [9]	A
Rom 1:16-17; 3:22b-28, (29-31)	Proper 4 [9]	A
Mt 7:21-29	Proper 4 [9]	A
Gn 12:1-9	Proper 5 [10]	A
Ps 33:1-12	Proper 5 [10]	A
Rom 4:13-25	Proper 5 [10]	A
Mt 9:9-13, 18-26	Proper 5 [10]	A
Gn 18:1-15, (21:1-7)	Proper 6 [11]	A
Ps 116:1-2, 12-19	Proper 6 [11]	A
Rom 5:1-8	Proper 6 [11]	A
Mt 9:35–10:8, (9-23)	Proper 6 [11]	A
Gn 21:8-21	Proper 7 [12]	A
Ps 86:1-10, 16-17	Proper 7 [12]	A
Rom 6:1b-11	Proper 7 [12]	A
Mt 10:24-39	Proper 7 [12]	A
Gn 22:1-14	Proper 8 [13]	A
Ps 13	Proper 8 [13]	A
Rom 6:12-23	Proper 8 [13]	A

Mt 10:40-42	Proper 8 [13]	A
Gn 24:34-38, 42-49, 58-67	Proper 9 [14]	A
Ps 45:10-17	Proper 9 [14]	A
Song 2:8-13 (Alt resp)	Proper 9 [14]	A
Rom 7:15-25a	Proper 9 [14]	A
Mt 11:16-19, 25-30	Proper 9 [14]	A
Gn 25:19-34	Proper 10 [15]	A
Ps 119:105-112	Proper 10 [15]	A
Rom 8:1-11	Proper 10 [15]	A
Mt 13:1-9, 18-23	Proper 10 [15]	A
Gn 28:10-19a	Proper 11 [16]	A
Ps 139:1-12, 23-24	Proper 11 [16]	A
Rom 8:12-25	Proper 11 [16]	A
Mt 13:24-30, 36-43	Proper 11 [16]	A
Gn 29:15-28	Proper 12 [17]	A
Ps 105:1-11, 45b (Alt)	Proper 12 [17]	A
Ps 128	Proper 12 [17]	A
Rom 8:26-39	Proper 12 [17]	A
Mt 13:31-33, 44-52	Proper 12 [17]	A
Gn 32:22-31	Proper 13 [18]	A

The Old Testament readings for Proper 4 through Proper 29 (which follow here) provide a pattern of paired readings in which the Old Testament and gospel readings are closely related. If a pattern of semicontinuous Old Testament readings is preferred, see pp. 90-92. The second reading and gospel are as indicated for each Proper above.

1 Jn 1:1–2:2	Easter 2	B
Jn 20:19-31	Easter 2	B
Acts 3:12-19	Easter 3	B
Ps 4	Easter 3	B
1 Jn 3:1-7	Easter 3	B
Lk 24:36b-48	Easter 3	B
Acts 4:5-12	Easter 4	B
Ps 23	Easter 4	B
1 Jn 3:16-24	Easter 4	B
Jn 10:11-18	Easter 4	B
Acts 8:26-40	Easter 5	B
Ps 22:25-31	Easter 5	B
1 Jn 4:7-21	Easter 5	B
Jn 15:1-8	Easter 5	B
Acts 10:44-48	Easter 6	B
Ps 98	Easter 6	B
1 Jn 5:1-6	Easter 6	B
Jn 15:9-17	Easter 6	B
Acts 1:1-11	Ascension	B
Ps 47	Ascension	B
Ps 93 (Alt)	Ascension	B
Eph 1:15-23	Ascension	B
Lk 24:44-53	Ascension	B
Acts 1:15-17, 21-26	Easter 7	B
Ps 1	Easter 7	B
1 Jn 5:9-13	Easter 7	B
Jn 17:6-19	Easter 7	B
Acts 2:1-21	Pentecost	B

Ez 37:1-14 (Alt)	Pentecost	B
Ps 104:24-34, 35b	Pentecost	B
Rom 8:22-27 (Alt)	Pentecost	B
Acts 2:1-21 (Alt)	Pentecost	B
Jn 15:26-27; 16:4b-15	Pentecost	B
Is 6:1-8	Trinity Sunday	B
Ps 29	Trinity Sunday	B
Rom 8:12-17	Trinity Sunday	B
Jn 3:1-17	Trinity Sunday	B

The Old Testament readings for Proper 4 through Proper 29 (which follow here) provide a pattern of semicontinuous Old Testament readings. If a pattern of paired readings is preferred, in which the Old Testament and gospel readings are closely related, see pp. 101-102. Since each pattern has its own consistency, it is important to select one or the other for use throughout the Sundays that follow Pentecost. For a discussion of these two approaches, see pp. 11 and 16-18 in the introduction.

1 Sam 3:1-10, (11-20)	Proper 4 [9]	B
Ps 139:1-6, 13-18	Proper 4 [9]	B
2 Cor 4:5-12	Proper 4 [9]	B
Mk 2:23–3:6	Proper 4 [9]	B
1 Sm 8:4-11, (12-15), 16-20, (11:14-15)	Proper 5 [10]	B

Ru 3:1-5; 4:13-17	Proper 27 [32]	B
Ps 127	Proper 27 [32]	B
Heb 9:24-28	Proper 27 [32]	B
Mk 12:38-44	Proper 27 [32]	B
1 Sm 1:4-20	Proper 28 [33]	B
1 Sm 2:1-10 (resp)	Proper 28 [33]	B
Heb 10:11-14 (15-18), 19-25	Proper 28 [33]	B
Mk 13:1-8	Proper 28 [33]	B
2 Sm 23:1-7	Reign of Christ [34]	B
Ps 132:1-12, (13-18)	Reign of Christ [34]	B
Rv 1:4b-8	Reign of Christ [34]	B
Jn 18:33-37	Reign of Christ [34]	B
Jl 2:21-27	Thanksgiving	B
Ps 126	Thanksgiving	B
1 Tm 2:1-7	Thanksgiving	B
Mt 6:25-33	Thanksgiving	B

The Old Testament readings for Proper 4 through Proper 29 (which follow here) provide a pattern of paired readings in which the Old Testament and gospel readings are closely related. If a pattern of semicontinuous Old Testament readings is preferred, see pp. 98-101. The second reading and gospel are as indicated for each Proper above.

Dt 5:12-15	Proper 4 [9]	B
Ps 81:1-10	Proper 4 [9]	B
Gn 3:8-15	Proper 5 [10]	B
Ps 130	Proper 5 [10]	B
Ez 17:22-24	Proper 6 [11]	B
Ps 92:1-4, 12-15	Proper 6 [11]	B
Jb 38:1-11	Proper 7 [12]	B
Ps 107:1-3, 23-32	Proper 7 [12]	B
Wis 1:13-15; 2:23-24	Proper 8 [13]	B
Lam 3:23-33 (Alt)	Proper 8 [13]	B
Ps 30	Proper 8 [13]	B
Ez 2:1-5	Proper 9 [14]	B
Ps 123	Proper 9 [14]	B
Am 7:7-15	Proper 10 [15]	B
Ps 85:8-13	Proper 10 [15]	B
Jer 23:1-6	Proper 11 [16]	B
Ps 23	Proper 11 [16]	B
2 Kgs 4:42-44	Proper 12 [17]	B
Ps 145:10-18	Proper 12 [17]	B
Ex 16:2-4, 9-15	Proper 13 [18]	B
Ps 78:23-29	Proper 13 [18]	B

Zep 3:14-20	Advent 3	C
Is 12:2-6 (resp)	Advent 3	C
Phil 4:4-7	Advent 3	C
Lk 3:7-18	Advent 3	C
Mi 5:2-5a	Advent 4	C
Lk 1:47-55	Advent 4	C
Ps 80:1-7 (Alt resp)	Advent 4	C
Heb 10:5-10	Advent 4	C
Lk 1:39-45, (46-55)	Advent 4	C
Is 9:2-7	Christmas Day 1	C
Ps 96	Christmas Day 1	C
Ti 2:11-14	Christmas Day 1	C
Lk 2:1-14, (15-20)	Christmas Day 1	C
Is 62:6-12	Christmas Day 2	C
Ps 97	Christmas Day 2	C
Ti 3:4-7	Christmas Day 2	C
Lk 2:(1-7), 8-20)	Christmas Day 2	C
Is 52:7-10	Christmas Day 3	C
Ps 98	Christmas Day 3	C
Heb 1:1-4, (5-12)	Christmas Day 3	C
Jn 1:1-14	Christmas Day 3	C
1 Sm 2:18-20, 26	Christmas 1	C
Ps 148	Christmas 1	C
Col 3:12-17	Christmas 1	C
Lk 2:41-52	Christmas 1	C

Nm 6:22-27	Holy Name	C
Ps 8	Holy Name	C
Gal 4:4-7	Holy Name	C
Phil 2:5-11 (Alt)	Holy Name	C
Lk 2:15-21	Holy Name	C
Eccl 3:1-13	New Year	C
Ps 8	New Year	C
Rv 21:1-6a	New Year	C
Mt. 25:31-46	New Year	C
Jer 31:7-14	Christmas 2	C
Sir 24:1-12 (Alt)	Christmas 2	C
Ps 147:12-20	Christmas 2	C
Wis 10:15-21 (Alt resp)	Christmas 2	C
Eph 1:3-14	Christmas 2	C
Jn 1:(1-9), 10-18	Christmas 2	C
Is 60:1-6	Epiphany	C
Ps 72:1-7, 10-14	Epiphany	C
Eph 3:1-12	Epiphany	C
Mt. 2:1-12	Epiphany	C
Is 43:1-7	Baptism of the Lord [1]	C
Ps 29	Baptism of the Lord [1]	C
Acts 8:14-17	Baptism of the Lord [1]	C
Lk 3:15-17, 21-22	Baptism of the Lord [1]	C
Is 62:1-5	Epiphany 2 [2]	C

Lk 13:31-35	Lent 2	C
Lk 9:28-36 (Alt)	Lent 2	C
Is 55:1-9	Lent 3	C
Ps 63:1-8	Lent 3	C
1 Cor 10:1-13	Lent 3	C
Lk 13:1-9	Lent 3	C
Jos 5:9-12	Lent 4	C
Ps 32	Lent 4	C
2 Cor 5:16-21	Lent 4	C
Lk 15:1-3, 11b-32	Lent 4	C
Is 43:16-21	Lent 5	C
Ps 126	Lent 5	C
Phil 3:4b-14	Lent 5	C
Jn 12:1-8	Lent 5	C
Lk 19:28-40 (palms)	Palm/Passion Sunday	C
Ps 118:1-2, 19-29 (palms)	Palm/Passion Sunday	C
Is 50:4-9a	Palm/Passion Sunday	C
Ps 31:9-16	Palm/Passion Sunday	C
Phil 2:5-11	Palm/Passion Sunday	C
Lk 22:14– 23:56	Palm/Passion Sunday	C
Lk 23:1-49 (Alt)	Palm/Passion Sunday	C
Is 42:1-9	Monday in Holy Week	C

Ps 36:5-11	Monday in Holy Week	C
Heb 9:11-15	Monday in Holy Week	C
Jn 12:1-11	Monday in Holy Week	C
Is 49:1-7	Tuesday in Holy Week	C
Ps 71:1-14	Tuesday in Holy Week	C
1 Cor 1:18-31	Tuesday in Holy Week	C
Jn 12:20-36	Tuesday in Holy Week	C
Is 50:4-9a	Wednesday in Holy Week	C
Ps 70	Wednesday in Holy Week	C
Heb 12:1-3	Wednesday in Holy Week	C
Jn 13:21-32	Wednesday in Holy Week	C
Ex 12:1-4, (5-10), 11-14	Holy Thursday	C
Ps 116:1-2, 12-19	Holy Thursday	C
1 Cor 11:23-26	Holy Thursday	C
Jn 13:1-17, 31b-35	Holy Thursday	C
Is 52:13–53:12	Good Friday	C
Ps 22	Good Friday	C
Heb 10:16-25	Good Friday	C
Heb 4:14-16, 5:7-9 (Alt)	Good Friday	C

Jn 18:1–19:42	Good Friday	C		Rom 6:3-11	Easter Vigil	C
				Ps 114	Easter Vigil	C
				Lk 24:1-12	Easter Vigil	C
Job 14:1-14	Holy Saturday	C				
Lam 3:1-9, 19-24 (Alt)	Holy Saturday	C				
				Acts 10:34-43	Easter	C
Ps 31:1-4, 15-16	Holy Saturday	C		Is 65:17-25 (Alt)	Easter	C
1 Pt 4:1-8	Holy Saturday	C		Ps 118:1-2, 14-24	Easter	C
Mt 27:57-66	Holy Saturday	C				
Jn 19:38-42 (Alt)	Holy Saturday	C		1 Cor 15:19-26	Easter	C
				Acts 10:34-43 (Alt)	Easter	C
Gn 1:1–2:4*a*	Easter Vigil	C		Jn 20:1-18	Easter	C
Ps 136:1-9, 23-26	Easter Vigil	C		Lk 24:1-12 (Alt)	Easter	C
Gn 7:1-5, 11-18, 8:6-18; 9:8-13	Easter Vigil	C		Is 25:6-9	Easter Evening	C
				Ps 114	Easter Evening	C
Ps 46	Easter Vigil	C		1 Cor 5:6*b*-8	Easter Evening	C
Gn 22:1-18	Easter Vigil	C		Lk 24:13-49	Easter Evening	C
Ps 16	Easter Vigil	C				
Ex 14:10-31; 15:20-21	Easter Vigil	C		Acts 5:27-32	Easter 2	C
Ex 15:1*b*-13, 17-18 (resp)	Easter Vigil	C		Ps 118:14-29	Easter 2	C
				Ps 150 (Alt)	Easter 2	C
Is 55:1-11	Easter Vigil	C		Rv 1:4-8	Easter 2	C
Is 12:2-6 (resp)	Easter Vigil	C		Jn 20:19-31	Easter 2	C
Bar 3:9-15, 32–4:4	Easter Vigil	C		Acts 9:1-6, (7-20)	Easter 3	C
Prv 8:1-8, 19-21; 9:4*b*-6 (Alt)	Easter Vigil	C		Ps 30	Easter 3	C
				Rv 5:11-14	Easter 3	C
Ps 19	Easter Vigil	C		Jn 21:1-19	Easter 3	C
Ez 36:24-28	Easter Vigil	C				
Ps 42 and 43	Easter Vigil	C				
Ez 37:1-14	Easter Vigil	C		Acts 9:36-43	Easter 4	C
Ps 143	Easter Vigil	C		Ps 23	Easter 4	C
Zep 3:14-20	Easter Vigil	C		Rv 7:9-17	Easter 4	C
Ps 98	Easter Vigil	C		Jn 10:22-30	Easter 4	C

Acts 11:1-18	Easter 5	C
Ps 148	Easter 5	C
Rv 21:1-6	Easter 5	C
Jn 13:31-35	Easter 5	C
Acts 16:9-15	Easter 6	C
Ps 67	Easter 6	C
Rv 21:10, 22–22:5	Easter 6	C
Jn 14:23-29	Easter 6	C
Jn 5:1-9 (Alt)	Easter 6	C
Acts 1:1-11	Ascension	C
Ps 47	Ascension	C
Ps 110 (Alt)	Ascension	C
Eph 1:15-23	Ascension	C
Lk 24:44-53	Ascension	C
Acts 16:16-34	Easter 7	C
Ps 97	Easter 7	C
Rv 22:12-14, 16-17, 20-21	Easter 7	C
Jn 17:20-26	Easter 7	C
Acts 2:1-21	Pentecost	C
Gn 11:1-9 (Alt)	Pentecost	C
Ps 104:24-34, 35b	Pentecost	C
Rom 8:14-17	Pentecost	C
Acts 2:1-21 (Alt)	Pentecost	C
Jn 14:8-17, (25-27)	Pentecost	C
Prv 8:1-4, 22-31	Trinity Sunday	C
Ps 8	Trinity Sunday	C

Rom 5:1-5	Trinity Sunday	C
Jn 16:12-15	Trinity Sunday	C

The Old Testament readings for Proper 4 through Proper 29 (which follow here) provide a pattern of semicontinuous Old Testament readings. If a pattern of paired readings is preferred, in which the Old Testament and gospel readings are closely related, see pp. 110-111. Since each pattern has its own consistency, it is important to select one or the other for use throughout the Sundays that follow Pentecost. For a discussion of these two approaches, see p. 11 in the introduction.

1 Kgs 18:20-21, (22-29), 30-39	Proper 4 [9]	C
Ps 96	Proper 4 [9]	C
Gal 1:1-12	Proper 4 [9]	C
Lk 7:1-10	Proper 4 [9]	C
1 Kgs 17:8-16, (17-24)	Proper 5 [10]	C
Ps 146	Proper 5 [10]	C
Gal 1:11-24	Proper 5 [10]	C
Lk 7:11-17	Proper 5 [10]	C
1 Kgs 21:1-10, (11-14), 15-21a	Proper 6 [11]	C
Ps 5:1-8	Proper 6 [11]	C
Gal 2:15-21	Proper 6 [11]	C
Lk 7:36–8:3	Proper 6 [11]	C
1 Kgs 19:1-4, (5-7),8-15a	Proper 7 [12]	C

1 Tm 1:12-17	Proper 19 [24]	C	Hb 1:1-4; 2:1-4	Proper 26 [31]	C
Lk 15:1-10	Proper 19 [24]	C	Ps 119:137-144	Proper 26 [31]	C
Jer 8:18–9:1	Proper 20 [25]	C	2 Thes 1:1-4, 11-12	Proper 26 [31]	C
Ps 79:1-9	Proper 20 [25]	C	Lk 19:1-10	Proper 26 [31]	C
1 Tm 2:1-7	Proper 20 [25]	C			
Lk 16:1-13	Proper 20 [25]	C	Dn 7:1-3, 15-18	All Saints	C
			Ps 149	All Saints	C
Jer 32:1-3a, 6-15	Proper 21 [26]	C	Eph 1:11-23	All Saints	C
Ps 91:1-6, 14-16	Proper 21 [26]	C	Lk 6:20-31	All Saints	C
1 Tm 6:6-19	Proper 21 [26]	C	Hg 1:15b–2:9	Proper 27 [32]	C
Lk 16:19-31	Proper 21 [26]	C	Ps 145:1-5, 17-21	Proper 27 [32]	C
Lam 1:1-6	Proper 22 [27]	C	Ps 98 (Alt resp)	Proper 27 [32]	C
Lam 3:19-26 (resp)	Proper 22 [27]	C	2 Thes 2:1-5, 13-17	Proper 27 [32]	C
Ps 137 (Alt resp)	Proper 22 [27]	C	Lk 20:27-38	Proper 27 [32]	C
2 Tm 1:1-14	Proper 22 [27]	C			
Lk 17:5-10	Proper 22 [27]	C	Is 65:17-25	Proper 28 [33]	C
			Is 12 (resp)	Proper 28 [33]	C
Jer 29:1, 4-7	Proper 23 [28]	C	2 Thes 3:6-13	Proper 28 [33]	C
Ps 66:1-12	Proper 23 [28]	C	Lk 21:5-19	Proper 28 [33]	C
2 Tm 2:8-15	Proper 23 [28]	C			
Lk 17:11-19	Proper 23 [28]	C	Jer 23:1-6	Reign of Christ [34]	C
Jer 31:27-34	Proper 24 [29]	C	Lk 1:68-79 (resp)	Reign of Christ [34]	C
Ps 119:97-104	Proper 24 [29]	C	Col 1:11-20	Reign of Christ [34]	C
2 Tm 3:14–4:5	Proper 24 [29]	C	Lk 23:33-43	Reign of Christ [34]	C
Lk 18:1-8	Proper 24 [29]	C			
Jl 2:23-32	Proper 25 [30]	C			
Ps 65	Proper 25 [30]	C	Dt 26:1-11	Thanksgiving	C
2 Tm 4:6-8, 16-18	Proper 25 [30]	C	Ps 100	Thanksgiving	C
Lk 18:9-14	Proper 25 [30]	C	Phil 4:4-9	Thanksgiving	C

Jn 6:25-35	Thanksgiving	C	Ps 25:1-10	Proper 10 [15]	C

The Old Testament readings for Proper 4 through Proper 29 (which follow here) provide a pattern of paired readings in which the Old Testament and gospel readings are closely related. If a pattern of semicontinuous Old Testament readings is preferred, see pp. 107-110. The second reading and gospel are as indicated for each Proper above.

			Gn 18:1-10a	Proper 11 [16]	C
			Ps 15	Proper 11 [16]	C
			Gn 18:20-32	Proper 12 [17]	C
			Ps 138	Proper 12 [17]	C
			Eccl 1:2, 12-14; 2:18-23	Proper 13 [18]	C
			Ps 49:1-12	Proper 13 [18]	C
1 Kgs 8:22-23, 41-43	Proper 4 [9]	C			
Ps 96:1-9	Proper 4 [9]	C	Gn 15:1-6	Proper 14 [19]	C
			Ps 33:12-22	Proper 14 [19]	C
1 Kgs 17:17-24	Proper 5 [10]	C	Jer 23:23-29	Proper 15 [20]	C
Ps 30	Proper 5 [10]	C	Ps 82	Proper 15 [20]	C
			Is 58:9b-14	Proper 16 [21]	C
2 Sm 11:26–12:10, 13-15	Proper 6 [11]	C	Ps 103:1-8	Proper 16 [21]	C
Ps 32	Proper 6 [11]	C	Sir 10:12-18	Proper 17 [22]	C
			Prv 25:6-7 (Alt)	Proper 17 [22]	C
Is 65:1-9	Proper 7 [12]	C	Ps 112	Proper 17 [22]	C
Ps 22:19-28	Proper 7 [12]	C			
			Dt 30:15-20	Proper 18 [23]	C
1 Kgs 19:15-16, 19-21	Proper 8 [13]	C	Ps 1	Proper 18 [23]	C
Ps 16	Proper 8 [13]	C			
			Ex 32:7-14	Proper 19 [24]	C
			Ps 51:1-10	Proper 19 [24]	C
Is 66:10-14	Proper 9 [14]	C			
Ps 66:1-9	Proper 9 [14]	C			
			Am 8:4-7	Proper 20 [25]	C
Dt 30:9-14	Proper 10 [15]	C	Ps 113	Proper 20 [25]	C

INDEX II

Scripture Readings Listed
According to the
Books of the Bible

Two symbols are used to indicate the two distinct patterns of Old Testament readings (and psalms) on the Sundays that follow Pentecost (Proper 4 through Proper 29). The symbol (+) indicates the pattern of semicontinuous Old Testament readings. The symbol (*) indicates the pattern of paired readings in which the Old Testament reading and the gospel reading are closely related. Since each pattern has its own consistency, it is important to select one or the other for use throughout the Sundays that follow Pentecost in a particular year.

Gn 1:1–2:4a	Trinity Sunday	A
Gn 1:1–2:4a	Easter Vigil	ABC
Gn 1:1–5	Baptism of the Lord [1]	B
Gn 2:15-17; 3:1-7	Lent 1	A
Gn 2:18-24*	Proper 22 [27]	B
Gn 3:8-15*	Proper 5 [10]	B
Gn 6:9-22; 7:24; 8:14-19	Proper 4 [9]	A
Gn 7:1-5, 11-18; 8:6-18; 9:8-13	Easter Vigil	ABC
Gn 9:8-17	Lent 1	B
Gn 11:1-9 (Alt)	Pentecost	C
Gn 12:1-4a	Lent 2	A
Gn 12:1-9+	Proper 5 [10]	A
Gn 15:1-6*	Proper 14 [19]	C
Gn 15:1-12, 17-18	Lent 2	C
Gn 17:1-7, 15-16	Lent 2	B

Gn 18:1-15, (21:1-17)+	Proper 6 [11]	A
Gn 18:1-10a*	Proper 11 [16]	C
Gn 18:20-32*	Proper 12 [17]	C
Gn 21:8-21+	Proper 7 [12]	A
Gn 22:1-14+	Proper 8 [13]	A
Gn 22:1-18	Easter Vigil	ABC
Gn 24:34-38, 42-49, 58-67+	Proper 9 [14]	A
Gn 25:19-34+	Proper 10 [15]	A
Gn 28:10-19a+	Proper 11 [16]	A
Gn 29:15-28+	Proper 12 [17]	A
Gn 32:22-31+	Proper 13 [18]	A
Gn 32:22-31*	Proper 24 [29]	C
Gn 37:1-4, 12-28+	Proper 14 [19]	A
Gn 45:1-15+	Proper 15 [20]	A
Gn 45:3-11, 15	Epiphany 7 [7]	C
Gn 50:15-21*	Proper 19 [24]	A